Dallasights

An Anthology of Architecture
and Open Spaces

American Institute of Architects
Dallas Chapter

Acknowledgments

Whenever a project of this magnitude is undertaken, countless people are involved. Many inevitably go unrecognized, though certainly not unappreciated; they know who they are, and to them we say thank you. There are a number of others whom I should like to single out. The authors of the essays spent countless hours of both office and leisure time to produce the text so vital to the book. Our copy editor, and my guru, Sally Wiley was remarkably accurate as well as indispensable. My personal compliments go to Jack Craycroft, AIA, who so cleverly maneuvered me into this position. The steady support of Past President Reagan George, AIA, and that of President Jerry Clement, AIA, have been quite comforting during those moments of doubt and indecision. We owe a sincere thank you to Nelson Spencer for giving us office space in The Quadrangle; a "permanent" temporary work area was vital once we reached the production stage. We are grateful to Emery Young, AIA, of Fort Worth for his assistance in assembling most of our photographs for that particular chapter. At least a thousand thank yous are extended to all the architects and their staffs who provided the essential photographs and information.

Everyone in the AIA Dallas Chapter owes Harris Kemp, FAIA, a sincere thank you and a hearty handshake. Without the fund raising of facile Harris, this book would still be a collection of unprinted art flats, loose photographs, and unedited essays.

The guidebook staff has been steadfast, reliable, and diligent in pursuit of the ultimate goal: a publication illustrating the built environment of Dallas that would make the architects and citizens of Dallas proud of their contributions. David Williams, Larry Good, and Gordon Gilmore are remarkable young men and the Dallas Chapter is greatly enriched by their membership.

We hope you enjoy the book and we hope our endeavors have produced a lasting treatise on Dallas, Texas, as it appeared in 1978.

This acknowledgment would be incomplete unless I thanked my wife Jan for her patience and understanding.

Alan R. Sumner, AIA

Staff

Editor	Alan R. Sumner, AIA
Staff	David K. Williams, AIA
	R. Lawrence Good, AIA
	Gordon K. Gilmore, AIA
	George A. Cole, AIA
	Stan Haas
Copy Editor	Sally Wiley

Contents

Authors

Toward a Living City
Weiming Lu — *M. Regional Planning, University of North Carolina; M.S. Civil Engineering, University of Minnesota* — is an Urban Design Program Manager for the Dallas Department of Urban Planning. Previously he was Chief of Environmental Design for the City of Minneapolis. He has been chairman of the Urban Design Department of the American Institute of Planners and a consulting member of AIA's Urban Design Committee. In 1977 the Texas Society of Architects made him an honorary member.

Growth, Planning & the CBD
Walter G. Dahlberg, ASLA — *B. S. Landscape Architecture, Texas A&M University* — is a principal in Myrick-Newman-Dahlberg, Inc., a firm engaged in urban design, planning, and landscape architecture both locally and as distant as Saudi Arabia. Significant projects he has been involved with include the Dallas/Fort Worth Regional Airport landscape plan, the master plan for Park Central, and planning for the ReUnion-Hyatt Regency Hotel.

Downtown Dallas —
The Moment Is at Hand
Vincent A. Carrozza — *B.A., Columbia University* — is managing partner of diverse real estate investment and development partnerships, several of which are active in Downtown Dallas. Carrozza has served on the Board of the Dallas Central Business District Association and on the Central Area Subcommittee of the Dallas City Planning Commission. He has been affiliated with such significant developments as Main Place and Dallas Centre.

Dallas Shops: Dry Goods Stores to Regional Malls
E. G. Hamilton, FAIA — *B. Architecture, Washington University* — is principal and director of design for Omniplan Architects Harrell+Hamilton. The firm has designed more than thirty department stores and has to its credit nine regional, enclosed-mall shopping centers. A number of them have garnered design awards. Hamilton is a past president of the AIA Dallas Chapter and of The National Council of Architectural Registration Boards.

A Selection of Parks
L. B. Houston — *B. S., Southern Methodist University* — was Director of Parks and Recreation for the city of Dallas from 1939 through 1972. He was awarded an Honorary Fellowship in the American Institute of Park Executives and served on the committee for the Secretary of the Interior's "Parks for America" program. Houston, a professional engineer and a registered landscape architect, also was a member of the Board of Trustees of the National Recreation and Park Association. Houston was awarded an Honorary Membership in the AIA Dallas Chapter and the Texas Society of Architects.

Fun and Sun in Dallas — A Review of Recreational Facilities
Dale E. Selzer, AIA — *B. S. Architectural Engineering, Ohio University;* is President of Selzer Associates, Inc., a firm that has won numerous design awards. Selzer has been active in the AIA serving as committee chairman, commissioner and an executive officer of the Dallas Chapter. An avid sportsman, Selzer has designed various recreational properties.

Plural Dwellings —
The Garden Apartment
Jack Craycroft, AIA — *B. S. Architectural Engineering, University of Texas* — is a principal with Craycroft-Lacy & Partners, a firm that has designed award winning multifamily housing projects. They currently have projects in twenty-nine states. In 1974 Craycroft was a juror for AIA Housing for Better Living, the AIA Houston design competition, and the AIA Austin design competition. He has served as AIA Dallas Chapter President and Director and as TSA Director.

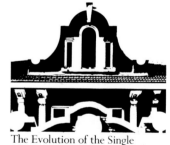

The Evolution of the Single Family House
James Wiley, AIA — *B. Architecture, Texas Tech University* — is a principal of The Oglesby Group, Inc., The firm has received numerous local and state design awards for a diversity of projects, several of which were residences. Wiley was a co-author of *The Prairie's Yield — Forces Shaping Dallas Architecture From 1840 to 1962,* and has served as an officer in the AIA Dallas Chapter, on the Dallas Urban Design Task Force, and on the Dallas Historic Landmark Committee.

Garden Office Buildings —
The Bottom Line
Jerrald L. Clement, AIA — *B. Architecture, University of Texas* — is the 1978 president of the AIA Dallas Chapter; he has been a member of the Building Code Advisory and Appeals Board of the City of Dallas. A principal of EDI/Cape/Hopkins/Clement/Guthrie Inc., Clement has been involved in designing a large number of garden office buildings. His firm has designed many other types of projects such as the shopping center Old Town in the Village, and Northlake Junior College.

The Multistory Office Building
Harwood K. Smith, AIA — *B. Architecture, Texas A&M University* — through his firm of Harwood K. Smith & Partners, has been designing multistory buildings for more than twenty years; there are nearly thirty of them scattered over various states. He is an active member of AIA and has served as Dallas Chapter President and Director. Smith, who attended the Chicago Art Institute, is an accomplished artist and has exhibited his watercolors nationwide.

Dallas — The Halls of Learning
Donald E. Jarvis, FAIA — *B. Architecture, Texas A&M University; M. Architecture, M.I.T.* — is president of Jarvis Putty Jarvis, a firm that has designed more than forty public-school projects and fourteen college and university buildings. A number of them have won local, state, or national awards. Besides being president of AIA Dallas and a director of TSA, Jarvis was the first chairman of the AIA Dallas Chapter's liaison committee to work with the Dallas Independent School District and was an Interim Planning Consultant to the DISD in connection with an $85 million bond program.

Houses of Worship
James A. Clutts, AIA — *B. Architecture, University of Texas; B. Structural Engineering, University of Kentucky* — a past president of AIA Dallas, has to his credit thirty-seven church projects, several of which have been cited by the Church Architecture Guild of America. Clutts has served on the executive committee of the Dallas Board of Church Extension of the United Methodist Church and as a member of the Board of the Greater Dallas Community of Churches. He is a principal in the firm Harper, Kemp, Clutts and Parker.

City and County Buildings
Terrell R. Harper, FAIA, FCSI — *Texas A&M University* — is a principal with Harper, Kemp, Clutts and Parker. He has been involved in the construction of a number of institutional and civic buildings; Harper and Kemp were associated architects for the new Dallas Municipal Administration Center. Harper was named a fellow by both AIA and the Construction Specifications Institute — a rare dual honor — and has served as president and director of AIA Dallas Chapter and as national president of CSI. He was a contributing author to the *Architect's Handbook of Professional Practice.*

Neighborhoods
R. Lawrence Good, AIA — *B. Architecture, University of Texas* — is an associate with Thompson/Parkey Associates. As a near-native of Dallas, he has been a special student of its neighborhood geography and sociology. Good is a staff member of *Dallasights,* has served on the Executive Committee for the AIA Dallas Chapter, and in 1977 was named "Young Architect of the Year" by AIA Dallas

Current Trends in Health Care
James S. Wright, AIA — *B. Architecture, Texas A&M University; M. Architecture, Cranbrook Academy of Art* — has been involved exclusively in health facilities planning for seventeen years. Wright is a senior partner with Page Southerland Page and a member of numerous professional organizations related to architecture for health. Recent projects include hospitals in Nigeria and Saudi Arabia and a medical school and teaching hospital in Taiwan.

Dallas — Showcase for the Nation
Ed E. Beran, AIA — *B. Architecture, University of Texas* — has been a partner in Beran & Shelmire since 1956. The firm's work includes the World Trade Center in Dallas and the Decorative Center in Houston. Several projects have received national attention. Beran has served the AIA Dallas Chapter as Treasurer. Currently he is president of the Texas Chapter of the Society of Architectural Historians.

Fair Park
Terrell R. Harper, FAIA, FCSI

Architecture for Industry: Dallas
David R. Braden, FAIA — *B. Architecture, University of Texas* — is chairman of Dahl/Braden/Chapman, Inc., a firm whose work includes more than a hundred manufacturing, distributing, and warehousing facilities throughout the nation. Braden has been president of both the AIA Dallas Chapter and the Texas Society of Architects, is on the Urban Design Task Force, and has long been involved in Goals for Dallas.

Fort Worth —
The Companion City
Alan R. Sumner, AIA — *B. Architecture, Texas Tech University* — is a principal in Greener & Sumner Architects, Inc., a firm that has designed projects in eleven states. He has served the AIA Dallas Chapter as an executive officer and commissioner. In 1975 the Dallas Chapter named him "Young Architect of the Year."

Dedication

This book was made possible in part by a grant from the National Gypsum Company. The Dallas Chapter of the American Institute of Architects extends a special acknowledgment to that company.

Very often it is only through the financial and moral support of companies like National Gypsum that AIA component chapters are able to publish compresensive documents on the architecture of their cities. By lending such support, those companies share in creating a historical record of the built environment of the United States. We sincerely thank the people of National Gypsum Company.

National Gypsum Company

Preface

Through numerous meetings of our original four-man committee, the concept for this publication slowly emerged. Our goal was to produce a photographic view of Dallas architecture and its open spaces, supported with essays by Dallas architects, planners, and businessmen. We agreed that it should be of the highest quality and that it would take an exclusive rather than an incluse approach to the architecture. In trying to focus on what is lasting and best, we have rejected the obviously mediocre, the bizarre, and the appalling — elements that can be seen in any large American city.

There has not been a comprehensive book on Dallas architecture since 1962, when *The Prairie's Yield* was published as the guide book for the AIA National Convention. Our city has developed dramatically during the past sixteen years. This is a record of those developments as well as a selective chronicle of our architecture, which began with the 1840 settlement on the Trinity River.

Dallas, like any city, must be experienced if its vitality is to be perceived and its atmosphere is to be felt. The photographs and essays only record; we hope they will stimulate the reader to seek out the City for himself. Chapter Three through Chapter Eleven separate the architecture into building types. The locations of the buildings, parks, or neighborhoods in each chapter are shown on introductory aerial maps. Using those maps and the essays, with a commercial city map, the reader can plan tours to suit his own particular interests.

Hundreds of photographs were submitted by the architects. Others were purchased or lent to AIA Dallas Chapter. More than two thousand photographs were taken by the staff to complement those submitted. With a few exceptions, all the uncredited photographs are by the staff.

The italicized text in the margins relates to the photographs on the page. Generally this text is assembled in the following order: name of the project; date of completion; architect; city, if the architect is not local; design awards; photo credit; and editorial comments. Although many of the architectural firms received a number of awards for design excellence, we elected to mention only those awards bestowed by AIA Dallas, by the Texas Society of Architects, and through programs sponsored by the National AIA. The familiar names of the architectural firms, rather than corporate or legal names, were used in crediting the projects.

The book is a selection of views of Dallas and its environs. Inherent in selection is value judgment. We hope our judgments will provoke the reader to think about and become sensitive to his heritage, both historic and recent. We also hope that in our effort to make a notable contribution to the City's and the Nation's record of man-made America we have been successful.

Chapter I
The City

Toward A Living City

Weiming Lu

Will Dallas become just another megalopolis? Or will it be a living city? Dallas's future, recognize it or not, is being shaped today.

Similarly, Dallas's today was shaped by decisions of yesterday. How a city came into being in the middle of a flat, hot, dry nowhere has more to do with human determination and creation than with historic reasons or geographic advantages.

Human creativity has made up for the geographic disadvantages. The railroads came and with them came more trade. The independent oil men chose to center here. Then came the insurance companies. The three early banks grew to giant institutions. The defense industries came, followed by electronics. Human vision has made possible the trade marts, where apparel and home furnishings are traded on an international scale. Tens of thousands lured by an abundance of jobs and a moderate climate have moved here.

Dallas still is a city on the move, where thousands of decisions are made by individuals and corporations that determine the city's form. Dallas has been built in a hurry. Dallas is a city of perpetual newness.

The phenomenal growth of the Southwest, the nationwide environmental movement, the energy crisis — all have made Dallas more and more aware that it must plan its future, and not, as in the past, simply let it happen. There is an increasing recognition that Dallas, despite its affluence, cannot afford to write off its downtown, to abandon its inner city. Dallas, despite its abundant land resources, cannot afford a haphazard use of its land, an insensitive management of its natural system. Land-use planning and environmental management have become new items on the City's agenda. Urban conservation has become a new concern for the community.

The need to shape the design of the city was first given public attention by the Goals for Dallas program in 1966. The expansion of the planning department in 1969 was based upon one of the recommendations in the Goals, and a direct result of that expansion was the creation in 1970 of an urban design division.

Urban design in Dallas helps to create urban forms and to manage urban growth. It deals with all aspects of urban life, from the sociology of the streets to the vitality of public spaces, from historic preservation to environmental management. It aims at both stabilizing the inner city and revitalizing downtown. It focuses upon the protection of the natural environment and upon the management of new growth in the outlying areas. Urban design is an integral part of the decision-making process of the City. The Dallas program includes not only the drawings, sketches, and models that make ideas perceivable, but also the legal instruments, financing devices, and administrative mechanisms that make ideas implementable.

The Dallas design staff collects data on the city environment and uses them as a basis for determining city programs for shaping urban growth. Natural and cultural systems have been documented by an ecological study, a visual form survey, and neighborhood environmental profiles. Landmarks have been identified and designated. Neighborhood meetings have been conducted regularly in various sections of the city to monitor and assess neighborhood needs and aspirations.

Above:
Photo: Kiku Obata

Left:
Photo: John Rhodes,
Dallas Morning News

Far left:
Photo: Greater Dallas Planning Council

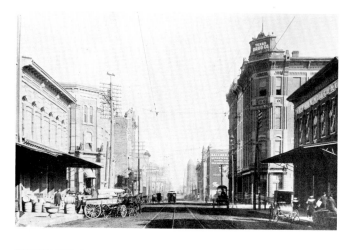

A data bank generated by the ecological study has formed a basis on which the design staff can work with developers, environmental groups, and public agencies in the area of environmental management. Earlier, the design staff, working with developers in the ecologically fragile Escarpment area, drew up guidelines for preventing soil erosion and protecting vegetation and proposed other building controls for a new, $200 million development in the southwest sector of the City. The developers in the area adopted the guidelines. Circulation plans and zoning proposals were refined to assure adequate regard for the environment. More recently, the design staff was asked to lead an interdepartmental and interdisciplinary team in the flood-plain study. Ecologically and hydrologically based guidelines for managing the flood plains were later adopted by the City Council. The Environmental Quality Committee has since its establishment received help from the design staff in monitoring the City's environment and in recommending citywide policies on environmental management and protection.

The City and the business community have become increasingly active in efforts to revitalize Downtown Dallas. The City Manager's office leads the city departments in those efforts. By improving the public spaces, by expanding convention and sport facilities, by joining in ventures with private interests, and more recently, by joining with art organizations in their planning, the City has helped to stimulate private investment in downtown.

One of the most ambitious efforts has been to acquire an abandoned railroad station, Union Terminal, and its site and to enter into a joint venture with private interests in developing a 50-acre, $210 million project that eventually will include a large hotel, offices, and a sports arena. The first phase, comprising the hotel and a 56-story observation tower, and the recycling of the railroad station, is well under way. The second phase, the sports and entertainment arena, is now being designed and scheduled for construction.

Another joint venture resulted in the completion of Thanks-Giving Square, a one-acre downtown park, designed by Philip Johnson, that has water, greenery, bell towers, and a chapel. A pedestrian concourse, retail spaces, and a truck terminal, all underneath the park, were parts of the project that the city design staff helped to design.

Already becoming a new monument for the city and creating a sense of place for that part of Downtown Dallas are the new City Hall and Civic Plaza, designed by I. M. Pei. In anticipation of the Central Research Library, now under construction, and the eventual expansion of the Federal Reserve Bank, the city design staff has developed a design framework around the new plaza.

In a strong commitment to preservation and revitalization, the City designated 55 acres of its old warehouse and county courthouse area as a Historic District. It imposed preservation criteria and height restrictions, reducing the allowable number of floors from twenty to eight, and committed itself to improving the public spaces. Private investors have already become involved in bringing more retail, office, and residential uses to the area, some of them renovating the facades and making other repairs, some of them completely reconstructing the buildings.

Other downtown improvements by the City — either built or contemplated — include creating boulevards and pedestrian malls, refining street signs, expanding and upgrading the Farmers Market, and controlling outdoor advertising.

Right:
Photo courtesy of Drury B. Alexander

In its efforts to conserve the inner city, the City has been active in neighborhood planning and areawide rezoning, and in promoting rehabilitation loans and grants as well as funds for capital improvements. Landmark preservation activities have been closely tied with neighborhood programs. The first historic district, Swiss Avenue, was designated in 1973. Since then it has attracted many new residents, and property values in the area continue to increase. This kind of conservation effort is now being applied to many other inner-city neighborhoods.

To encourage the reclamation of older neighborhoods, revolving funds for preservation purposes — funds guaranteed by the City — have been set up under Community Development Block Grants. Building codes have been studied to see how they can be safely revised to accommodate historic preservation; some changes are now being implemented. A preservation plan is being prepared. A federation of preservation groups has just been formed, signalling that the preservation movement has become citywide.

In the interest of encouraging private entities to build housing for middle- and higher-income families in the inner city, the City has come up with an innovative "area redevelopment program." Under the program, the City assists the prospective developer by rezoning, by making street adjustments and utility improvements, and most importantly by guaranteeing to buy back the land at a given price if he fails to realize his plan. The risks to the developer are thus reduced and the City is spared the cost of a massive urban-renewal bureaucracy. Currently a developer is involved in the preliminary stages of an eighty-acre, $85 million project under the program.

With the leadership of the Mayor, the City Council, and the City Manager, the City has persuaded the principal art organizations in Dallas to join it in developing and financing a comprehensive art-facilities planning study. The planning process, though complicated and precarious, has been successfully carried out, and some difficult decisions on facilities and sites have been made. Before long, public funding and private contributions will help to realize the comprehensive plan, which includes, among other facilities, a new art museum to be designed by Edward Larabee Barnes, an old vaudeville theater to be renovated by The Oglesby Group for various performing arts, a new symphony hall with Cyrus Harris as acoustician, and a new theater by Kenzo Tange. The art organizations in Dallas are stronger than ever, and their programs and activities enrich most profoundly the lives of all Dallasites.

Dallas, like other large cities, spends a great deal on street and highway improvements. To make the most of that investment, the City has developed better design standards for street hardware and landscaping, made greater efforts to enforce the new sign ordinance, and improved the design of traffic and information signs.

The preparation of a new sign ordinance for Dallas was one of the most challenging jobs of urban design. It took the city two and a half years to review sign problems and to develop new concepts in sign regulation. Gaining public support was equally time consuming. The result was a performance-based sign ordinance, completed and adopted in 1973.

The list of activities involving urban design is constantly changing and growing, but the basic objectives remain the same: urban conservation and an environment of the highest quality. Dallas is achieving these objectives through day-to-day design actions, and those actions are based on a consciousness of an encompassing citywide plan. A formal citywide design for Dallas has yet to be drawn up. But the City already has vital components such as the historic preservation plan, the art facilities plan, citizen-designated Goals for the Design of the City, and basic inventories of ecology and visual form; clearly, it is in a splendid position to launch such an effort.

Dallas's design activities have three basic characteristics, (1) a comprehensive approach, (2) interdisciplinary teamwork, and (3) active citizen involvement.

Citizens are increasingly aware that the quality of the environment is closely related to the quality of life they enjoy. They demand more response from city government and a commitment to solving diverse environmental problems. The only way to respond to such a wide range of urban problems is through a comprehensive approach. The answer to a specific problem often lies not in a specific solution. It may lie instead in the combined effects of a number of interrelated solutions to a cluster of specific problems. When urban conservation measures, for example, are closely linked with landmark preservation, it is possible to save the past and at the same time make the past serve the present. When flood-plain management is tied in with open-space planning, it is possible to achieve the goals of both.

To deal with a diversity of issues, expertness in a variety of disciplines — architecture, ecology, behavioral science, economics, law — may be required. The wisest solutions may derive from interdisciplinary teamwork.

Citizens are encouraged to participate in every urban design activity of the City. Generally speaking, two levels of participation are essential. First is the broad participation by all elements of the community in a general goal-setting endeavor such as the Goals for Dallas program. A sense of community has been generated by that program, and an over-all direction for Dallas has emerged. By being actively involved in the Goals process, the urban design staff has been able to learn more about the public's needs and aspirations and to put design and environmental issues in the public arena for discussion and adoption.

A second level of participation involves groups interested in specific issues (such as the sign ordinance) or neighborhoods facing specific problems (such as Little Mexico). The design staff brings groups together and helps them arrive at workable solutions. The process is often long, but the result is always vital to neighborhood improvement.

Center:
Photo: David Woo,
Dallas Morning News

Cyclist:
Photo: John Rhodes,
Dallas Morning News

Tennis player:
Photo: Courtesy Dallas Chamber
of Commerce

Above:
Photo: Larry Reese,
Dallas Morning News

Right:
Photo: David Woo,
Dallas Morning News

Dallas has been fortunate to have active and visionary civic leadership and broad community support. Vital to the progress of the City have been such diverse organizations as Goals for Dallas, Save Open Space, the Chambers of Commerce, the Central Business District Association, neighborhood associations, the American Institute of Architects, the American Society of Landscape Architects, the American Institute of Planners, the League of Women Voters, the Historic Preservation League, and the Dallas County Heritage Society.

The financial support that Dallas has given its urban design program in the last six years has averaged about 25 cents per citizen per year. While it is difficult to measure the impact of such activities in so short a time, it is clear that the investment in design has been repaid many times over in economic, social, and environmental gains. Urban design has helped to project a new image for City Hall and to provide a new vision for City Management.

Landmark preservation and neighborhood conservation have helped the community realize its inner-city potential. In a number of neighborhoods, families have moved back and property values have stabilized or increased. It is even possible that a back-to-the-city movement has begun in Dallas.

City governments everywhere have been challenged to assume new and greater responsibilities, but their fiscal resources have not increased proportionately. They must, therefore, use what resources they have more sensitively and more effectively. Dallas is no exception. If this city is to meet such challenges, as Dallas City Manager George Schrader pointed out recently in a speech before the National Conference of the American Institute of Planners, three things are crucial:

"First, there must be an effective decision-making process in the community so that issues may be raised, discussed, and resolved. Energetic leadership and broad community participation are indispensable. Balanced consideration must be given to environmental interests and business interests. Open and meaningful dialogue between the two should be nurtured, and trade-offs should be facilitated.

"Second, city improvement programs should be carefully coordinated through an effective urban design process. Urban design, to be useful today, must be both 'policy oriented' so that, along with social, economic, and physical-design goals, it can be tied to the City's long-range growth strategy, and 'action oriented' so that it can serve as a basis for formulating capital improvement programs. Above all, those programs should directly or indirectly help to enrich Dallas's environment.

"Third, there must be a professional management team — of which the urban design staff is a member — to provide innovative and energetic leadership and to see that the City's programs are continuously responsive to the needs and aspirations of the public."

While much has been accomplished in the past years in neighborhood conservation, downtown renewal, historic preservation, and environmental management, much remains to be done. New problems are already emerging. New goals are now being formed. A new agenda for the city is urgently needed. It should include the following:

A strategy for implementing a more energy-efficient transportation system.

An open-space system planned and developed on the basis of projected growth trends, population profiles, leisure time activities, and natural ecology.

A strategy for achieving optimum growth for the area without sacrificing the quality of the environment.

New zoning and subdivision ordinances that will simplify procedures, reduce delays, permit the free application of modern land planning, consider economics, ecology, and energy, and allow for security, privacy, and neighborhood identity.

A comprehensive strategy for downtown that will make it attractive and hospitable to all people of all ages at all times for a multitude of functions and pleasures.

A keener appreciation of historic preservation and neighborhood conservation efforts and an understanding of the individual needs of specific areas of the city.

The development of strong local leadership so that grass-roots energy can be used to improve inner-city neighborhoods.

City government today has a responsibility beyond that of efficiency and integrity; it fulfills its true function only when it acts with a sense of excellence and a concern for aesthetic values.

We can make our city as sterile as poorly planned subdivisions and as barren as concrete pavement. But to do so is to degrade man's spirit and to kill the impulse to creativity. We can, on the other hand, broaden our concerns and help to fulfill the highest function of city government by recognizing in long-range policy decisions and in day-to-day actions the need to bring the outside man-made world into harmony with the inner needs of the individual. We must concern ourselves with the shape of urban growth and with the quality of the urban environment. Through creative urban design we reach beyond utility and necessity in city living and seek to attain in some measure the ideal of a living city.

The views expressed in this essay are those of the author; they may or may not represent those of the City.

Photo: Larry Reese,
Dallas Morning News

Chapter 2
Central Business District

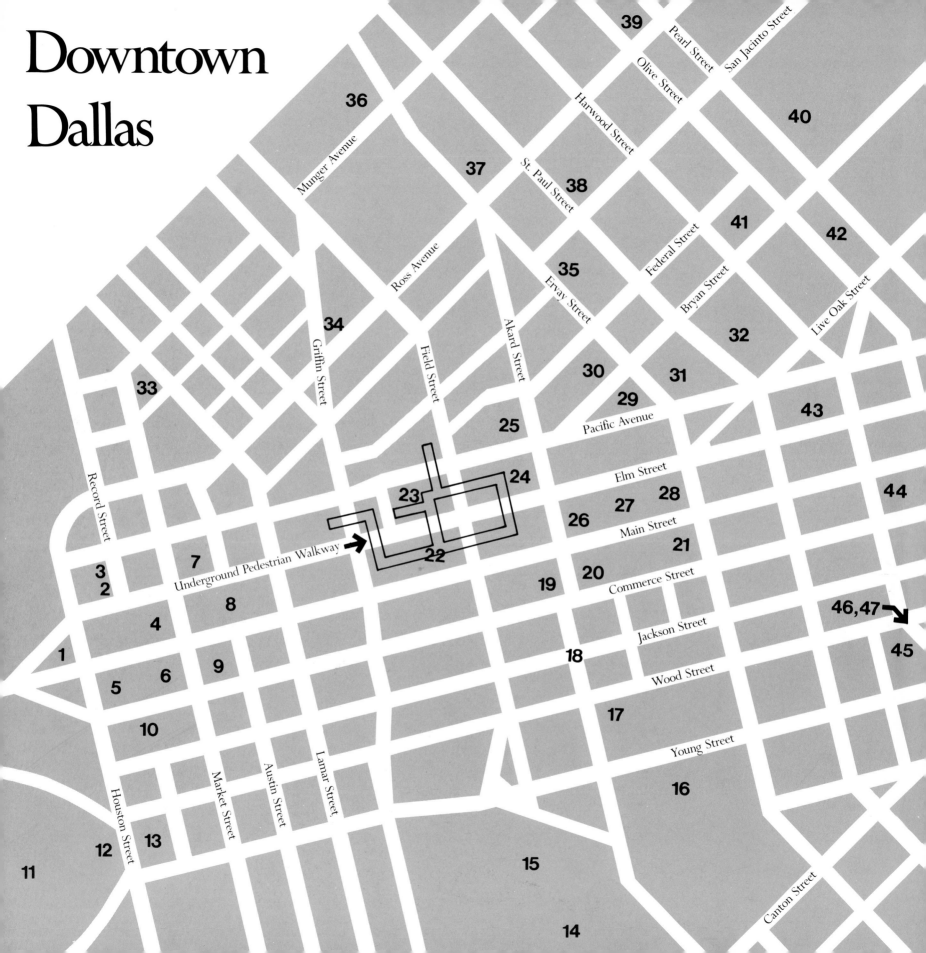

Downtown Dallas

Munger Avenue

Ross Avenue

Griffin Street

Field Street

Akard Street

Ervay Street

St. Paul Street

Harwood Street

Olive Street

Pearl Street

San Jacinto Street

Federal Street

Bryan Street

Live Oak Street

Record Street

Pacific Avenue

Elm Street

Main Street

Commerce Street

Jackson Street

Wood Street

Young Street

Canton Street

Houston Street

Market Street

Austin Street

Lamar Street

Underground Pedestrian Walkway

36 37 38 39 40 41 42

35 34 33 32 43

30 31 29 25 24 23 22 28 27 26 21 20 19 44 46,47 45

7 3 2 8 4 1 6 5 9 10 18 17 16 15 14 12 13 11

Photo: Doug Tomlinson

John Neely Bryan Cabin in the Dallas County Historical Plaza

Growth, Planning, and the CBD

Walter G. Dahlberg, ASLA

Young Street Urban Design Study 1975 Myrick-Newman-Dahlberg, Planners With the construction in the mid-70s of the new City Hall, the Dallas Convention Center, and ReUnion, Young Street became a significant promenade at the southern edge of the urban core.

Dallas is a unique city with a unique history. It did not "happen" through historical accident, as many cities do, nor through unusual natural advantages. It came about through the pioneer spirit of John Neely Bryan, who shall be called the original speculator of North Texas. In the development of the city, the *pioneer spirit* has been maintained, over-shadowed only by the *speculator spirit* — a marriage of the two spirits is what makes Dallas thrive. Its growth from a trading post on the Trinity to an internationally famous city in little more than a century and a quarter reflects the action-charged personality of "Big D."

Milestones in the City's development from the time of its founding in 1846 are the arrival of the first railroad in 1872, the establishment of the State Fair of Texas in 1886, the consolidation with Oak Cliff in 1903, the founding of the Dallas Cotton Exchange in 1907 and of Southern Methodist University in 1915, the development of the Convention Center in 1957 and its expansion in 1975, and the recent planning and construction of the architecturally outstanding new City Hall. The next great stride — the redevelopment on a large scale of the inner city — is exemplified by the Reunion-Hyatt Regency project and the Reunion Central Park Development, to be completed in 1978; the proposed Plaza of the Americas Hotel and retail center; and perhaps even more important, the Fox and Jacobs project. The last of these is an effort by local developers to reclaim a large tract of land at the edge of the Central Business District for inner-city middle-income housing.

Dallas has a strong, highly diversified economy; the number of million-dollar corporations within the metropolitan area exceeds a thousand. It is headquarters for five of the state's top ten corporations. In addition, Dallas is the financial center of Texas: It is headquarters for the 11th Federal Reserve District and is home for the largest bank in the Southwest. The population of the Dallas metropolitan area, 2.7 million, places it tenth in the nation.

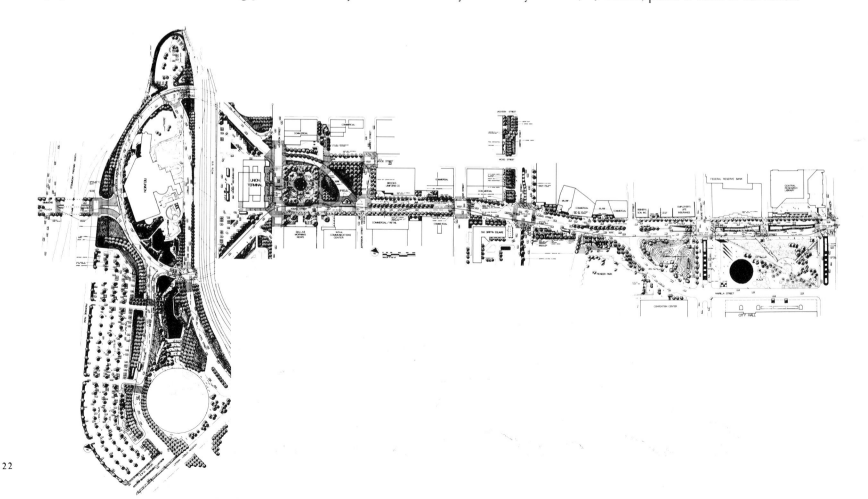

The Dallas story has been written again and again — sometimes accurately, sometimes with a degree of abandon. For the curious there are several publications worth looking into. Two early ones are John Henry Brown's *History of Dallas County, Texas, From 1837 to 1887* (published 1887) and Philip Lindsley's *A History of Greater Dallas and Vicinity* (published 1909). A more recent volume is *The Lusty Texans of Dallas* (1951), by John William Rogers. In contrast with those is a large, colorful 1973 publication, A. C. Greene's *Dallas, The Deciding Years — A Historical Portrait*. Look for this in the local bookstores and then get A. C. to autograph it for posterity. A small book of high quality is *The Prairie's Yield — Forces Shaping Dallas Architecture From 1840 to 1962*. This was written by members of the American Institute of Architects, Dallas Chapter, for distribution at the 1962 AIA National Convention. Copies are difficult to obtain, but the book is useful and deserves to be republished. An interesting document on both people and places in Dallas is *The Book of Dallas, 1976*, by Evelyn Oppenheimer and Bill Porterfield.

Stone Place 1965, formerly a street, is a short pedestrian mall in the very heart of downtown. Connecting Elm and Main Streets, it serves as a small park for office workers.

Upper left:
First National Bank 1965
George L. Dahl and Thomas E. Stanley, Joint Venture Architects

Lower left:
The Skyline at dusk: The mirrored facade of ReUnion's Hyatt Regency Hotel catches the last rays of the setting sun.
Photo: Courtesy Woodbine Corp.

The Texas Centennial peristyle in Dealey Plaza and "Old Red", the Richardsonian Romanesque County Courthouse, stand guard at the western entrance to the CBD.
Photo: Dan Barsotti

Belo Mansion 1890
Architect unknown.
Photo: Bill Hendricks
This house, built by the founder of The Dallas Morning News, has been placed on the National Register of Historic Places.

Dominating all the historical facts about Dallas is *growth*. For better or worse, richer or poorer, planned or unplanned — growth. It began in 1846 with John Neely Bryan's 580-acre grant from the Peters Colony and hasn't stopped. Bryan started with a plan. His town was laid out in a grid-iron pattern, in blocks 200 feet square, the main streets running east and west, the cross streets north and south, or almost; they were oriented slightly off the cardinal points of the compass. As Bryan's town grew, it encountered another parcel, that of John Grigsby, which had been surveyed but not developed. Grigsby's plotting was 30° out of alignment with Bryan's. The two street systems persisted and have both plagued and enhanced the city. The discontinuity of streets is an annoyance; but the strange shapes of blocks have provided interesting design opportunities, and odd, triangular parcels have been turned into parks and landscaped setbacks.

People and goods moved by horseback and oxcart and stagecoach and Dallas prospered. Then the town leaders said "We need railroads." So in the early 1870s the railroads came — by dint of some heavy-handed political persuasion (much as roads and highways are now built to accommodate the speculator: What's good for the landowner must be good for the city). For moving about town there was the streetcar. By 1879 Dallas had more than 70 miles of track.

(None of it remains; what hasn't been dug up is now covered with brick and asphalt.)

With the railroads came more prosperity and more growth. But that growth was essentially unplanned, unorchestrated. There was no thought for what we would now call an infrastructure. The spirit of the utilitarian grid prevailed. Development continued, over the farmlands and into the river bottoms. Chaos came with the horseless carriage and tragedy with the 1908 flood. The Trinity River caused 1.5 million dollars' worth of damage to construction in the flood plain (unfortunately, we don't seem to have profited by their mistakes).

In a brief sobering-up period a civic organization was formed, the Dallas City Plan and Improvement League. Two outgrowths of that League have had a lasting effect on Dallas. One was that George E. Kessler of Kansas City and St. Louis was retained in 1910 to deal with the unbridled growth that had forever characterized the City; from him came the first comprehensive city plan, the Kessler Plan. The other was that a new bridge, the Oak Cliff Viaduct, was constructed over the Trinity, joining Dallas to the west bank and opening that part of the City to further expansion. The viaduct, now known as the Houston Street Viaduct, was at the time reputed, in typical Dallas spirit, to be the longest concrete structure in the world.

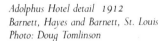

As with any city at any time, there are the dreamers and there are the doers, and only rarely are they the same persons. At the turn of the century, with a population close to 100,000, Dallas needed what the Kessler Plan envisioned. But the doers considered his scheme too grand and too utopian, and little of it was carried out. It was not until the 1930s that even so basic and vital an element of the Plan as levees for the Trinity came into being. A part of the Plan that did materialize, Turtle Creek Parkway, remains one of the City's greatest assets. Other manifestations of the Plan, either direct or indirect, are Ferris Plaza in front of Union Terminal, and Dealey Plaza, the entrance to the City from the west. The Kessler Plan seems less and less far-fetched, and from time to time it is still referred to by dreamers and planners. Long live a plan, any plan — for some sort of plan is better than no plan at all.

A concert in Akard Street Mall
Photo: Ron Underwood

Far right:
Akard Street Mall 1976
Myrick-Newman-Dahlberg, Planners

Right:
Republic Bank and the Chapel of
Thanks-Giving

Scottish Rite Temple 1907
Photo: Courtesy of
Drury B. Alexander

But the CBD went on its independent way. Building eclectically and willy-nilly, and willy-nilly tearing down. There was a succession of superlatives: the Adolphus Hotel, Beaux Arts design pushed to its limits; the Busch Building (now the United National Bank Building), a seminal example of the Gothic skyscraper; the Union Terminal, with its white glazed brick facade — fallout from the Chicago World's Fair — and the grandest space south of Kansas City; the Magnolia Building (now the Mobil Building) with its revolving red horse, in 1921 the tallest building west of the Mississippi; the Medical Arts Building, in 1923 the world's tallest reinforced concrete structure; the Mercantile Bank Building, built just before World War II, another "tallest building west of the Mississippi"; the Republic National Bank with, in 1954, the fastest curtain wall in the West; the Southland Center, yet another tallest building this side of the Big River, and the first in Dallas to define its mass with nighttime lighting, a practice that has become something of a Dallas tradition.

In the late 1920s and 1930s, while the speculators and the empire builders were one-upping each other, nothing much was happening in the way of planning. But by the 1940s it became clear that things were getting out of hand. To develop a Comprehensive Master Plan, the City retained Hare and Hare, Landscape Architects, and Harlan Bartholomew and Associates, City Planners. In their plans they iterated much of Kessler's vision, adding also a civic center in the heart of the city. The idea was to build the City Beautiful. But little of it materialized, the City Beautiful giving way to the City Efficient. In the 1960s the City hired Ponte-Travers Associates as planning and traffic consultants. They presented their recommendations in late 1969. Their proposals included a grade-separated pedestrian network, new downtown parks and green spaces, revised street systems and improved streetscapes, a transit system, and an underground truck and service system. Actual progress has been made on that plan, and there are visible signs in the inner city to prove it.

In 1965 a great step was taken to put some of the planning in the hands of the people. Erik Jonsson, then mayor of the City of Dallas, put to the citizens this challenge:

"Shall we deal adequately with the future or be run over by it? . . . We must dream no small dreams. We must envision great, ambitious, difficult goals. Yet our objectives must be within our reach."

Thus Goals for Dallas was born. It was an intensive effort to involve everyone, either personally or by representative, in the development of a comprehensive program. Hundreds of citizens came together to draw up specific objectives, to set priorities, and to determine how to achieve them. (By 1976 the vast majority of those objectives had been met, so the call went out again, and the process was repeated.) An outgrowth of the 1965 Goals for Dallas was a restructuring of the Department of Urban Planning and the development of a Division of Urban Design. One of the subject areas of the Goals is The Design of the City. A goal of The Design of the City prompted the establishment of the Urban Design Task Force. The purpose of the Task Force, which consists of architects, landscape architects, planners, engineers, and laymen, is to assist City entities in reviewing matters that involve urban design. Outstanding among the accomplishments of the Task Force was its persuading the City to hire Weiming Lu, formerly Chief of Environmental Design for Minneapolis. In 1971 he was brought in to head the new Division of Urban Design.

At last, an integrated approach to urban planning began to show itself. One of the first results was the transformation (by Myrick-Newman-Dahlberg, Landscape Architects) of four blocks of Akard Street into a quasi-pedestrian mall linking the heart of the business district with the Convention Center and the new City Hall, and incidentally enhancing the setting of the flamboyant Adolphus Hotel. The faltering Thanks-Giving Square project was given new life. Other first fruits were new street graphics and a new sign ordinance. Computerized banks of data on the environment were set up to help city departments, the City Plan Commission, and the City Council in making decisions about the built environment.

In 1973 a Historic Landmark Preservation Ordinance was passed, and a section of Swiss Avenue was declared a Historic District. Shortly afterwards Drury B. Alexander was engaged to make a survey of potential historic landmarks in the city. His report to the city (submitted in September 1974) included a review of what he felt were Dallas's more valuable assets and a list of those landmarks that on a local, state, or national basis merit conserving. Listed as being particularly important was an area long known as the Old Warehouse District. Few of the low red brick buildings are significant in themselves, but as a group they convey a sense of the times when they were the heart of the City's commerce. The area was declared a Historic Subdistrict in 1976.

Left:
Kingman-Texas Implement Co. 1902
(now John F. Kennedy Museum)
Hubbell and Greene
Located in the historic Warehouse District, this building was among the city's first Chicago School Skyscrapers
Photo: Doug Tomlinson

Lower left:
Purse & Co. Building c. 1910
J. A. Padgitt
Photo: Doug Tomlinson

The significance of Thanks-Giving Square as valuable open space is evident, as these office buildings stretch for a view.

It remains to be seen how the City and the citizens act upon other recommendations in the Alexander report. The very vitality that has built Dallas is what has caused it to lose the outward and visible signs of its history. Only extraordinary tenacity on the part of sensitively sensible people can retain for its citizens, present and future, what little remains of a visible continuity of the City's development.

The most ambitious planning effort of recent years has been a comprehensive land-use plan. In a region where "my granddaddy settled this land and, By God, it's mine to do with as I please," such a plan meets opposition. Again and again it goes down in defeat; speculation and the pioneer attitude prevail. But the times declare that a broadly encompassing plan is more than valid: It is essential. So again and again it surfaces.

On the whole, the character of Dallas design has been infused with a Middle-Western stolidity — conservative, somewhat lacking in excitement. But both architecture and planning here have begun to take a turn. There are among the city leaders, as well as the citizens as a whole, a growing appreciation of the arts, a more sophisticated sense of aesthetics, and an awareness that a cohesive plan is needed for dealing with urban concerns. The City is enjoying a boom of economic and physical growth, and much of that boom is taking place in the center of the city.

There has been a turnabout in population movement. Areas bounded by Loop 12 that for years were in a steady decline are suddenly highly desirable. Housing prices soar as people move back from the outer suburbs. Young, first-time home owners are willing to live in an older neighborhood in order to be closer in. Even townhouses and condominiums, so antithetical to the frontier spirit, are not merely accepted but sought after as places to live nearer the city.

The present Central Business District is a good base on which to develop all the amenities necessary for a complete urban environment. The creation of downtown facilities for the visual and performing arts, new theaters, hotels, a sports arena, the proposed Town Lake — all of which are at least on the drawing boards — will make downtown living even more appealing. Much is being planned for Downtown Dallas to make it enjoyable and enticing. Landscaped pedestrianways — malls, arcades, plazas, concourses, small parks — are being developed to connect apartment buildings and hotels with nearby facilities, improving pedestrian movement and providing some separation from automobile traffic. With all the present and planned activity, with a strong potential market, and with available land, the time is ripe for new near-town residential development. The existing need for downtown housing is estimated at four thousand units, projected to six thousand by 1980.

Moving to Dallas in increasing numbers are people, unencumbered by frontier prejudices, who are accustomed to being in the heart of the city. They perceive and demand the advantages: the proximity to work and to cultural and civic life; the satisfaction of walking rather than depending completely on the automobile; the exhilaration of a bustling atmosphere. They could have what they want. At this very moment there is a spark in Downtown Dallas such as the City has rarely seen. It needs only to be fanned.

Downtown Dallas—The Moment Is at Hand

Vincent A. Carrozza

The question is often posed whether it is more difficult to develop downtown property or property in the suburbs. The response must be that, even when the competition with suburban office space has been less intense than it is now, it has always been more arduous to develop real estate downtown. Land is more expensive and far more difficult, because of its fractured ownership, to obtain. The street system and utility network present special constrictions and call upon disciplines that are not involved in outlying development.

Those problems have been exacerbated by recent changes in the marketing and financing of downtown projects.

The single office building on a narrow plot of land is fast becoming obsolete. Taking its place is the large "mixed use" development that combines office, hotel, retail, restaurant, and recreational facilities. And the lenders — the large ones — keenly aware of the long-term values of such an arrangement, are far more enthusiastic about financing that kind of project than they are about financing the lone office building whose environment cannot be controlled.

This emphasis on larger projects brings with it a call for larger tracts of land — a formidable problem not only because of the difficulty of acquiring the rights to it (To create Main Place in Dallas, ten years were consumed in obtaining title to ten acres of land. There were ninety parcels involved, and four hundred signatures.), but also because, increasingly, land can be acquired only by long-term ground lease. Conforming ground leases to the long-term requirements of lenders is a troublesome, frustrating, and often very expensive enterprise, particularly when the lease has open-ended escalation provisions.

As the fashion for bridging streets to adjoining property heightens, the cost of skirting or removing utilities must be added to the total cost.

The costs of construction on the narrower downtown building sites are increased also by the lack of space for storing building material.

Offsetting those negative aspects is the positive fact that there are countless office users who refuse to be anywhere but downtown. The market for downtown office space in Dallas has grown at a formidable rate since 1950: The demand has increased by an average of 500,000 square feet per year.

The structural cross-bracing of the First International Building is expressed only at night. The lighting carries on the Dallas tradition of downtown buildings defining their mass through dramatic nighttime lighting.
Photo: Barbara Martin

Downtown Dallas by 1990 may benefit from a Town Lake (upper left in photo). The lake would lie between the levees within the existing floodway of the Trinity River.
Drawing: Steve Winslow

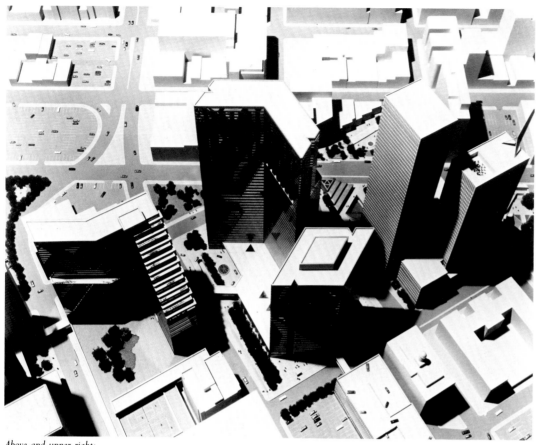

Above and upper right:
Dallas Centre, under construction 1978
I. M. Pei & Partners, New York;
Fisher & Spillman, Associated Architects.
One is reminded of Pei's John Hancock
Tower in Boston.

Far right & Facing page:
Plaza of the Americas, proposed, 1978
Harwood K. Smith & Partners
Twin 25-story office towers and 15-floor
hotel are clustered around a retail atrium
space and ice chalet.

Right & facing page:
ReUnion-Hyatt Regency Hotel and
Observation Tower
Welton Becket & Associates, Los Angeles.
Photos: Courtesy Woodbine Corp.
With the renovation of Union Terminal,
these form Phase One of the ReUnion
project. (The name was derived from La
Reunion, a short-lived utopian colony of
European settlers founded near Dallas in
1856.)

Beyond that, however, Downtown Dallas, historically strong as a national convention center, is about to spring forth as one of America's most interesting cities in the quality of its architecture and the variety of experiences it can offer.

In the public sector we now have the I. M. Pei City Hall, a symbol of our city whose design has already won world-wide acclaim. We have also seen started the 40-million-dollar Central Research Library. Before long we shall see an indoor-sports and entertainment arena and a new Dallas Museum of Fine Arts, eventually perhaps a Symphony Hall and the remodeling of the Majestic Theater. For the fringe of the downtown area a sixty- to eighty-acre housing development is being planned. Within the downtown area there are now under way several mixed-use developments, including the 200-million-dollar Dallas Centre and the nearly completed first phase of the Reunion project.

With the introduction of nighttime cultural, educational, and recreational activities we can forecast the opening of more high-quality restaurants. All of those will spur the development of housing — from apartment towers to townhouses — within the downtown loop of freeways.

The synergism resulting from those complementary and supporting uses will lead to a renascence that, in my opinion, promises to reconstruct Downtown Dallas into one of this country's most exciting and satisfying places.

To return to the original question, What kind of property is more difficult to develop? The answer is obvious. But at this time and in this place there is a sense of excitement and anticipation that the future is at hand and that unless we seize this fleeting moment the opportunity may be lost forever.

Chapter 3
Commerce

*The four buildings of The Sanger Bros.
Department Store complex reflected the
early development of skyscraper style in
Dallas, from the Richardsonian
Romanesque of Security Mortgage and
Trust to the Louis Sullivan-inspired
Sangers Store of 1910 by Lang &
Witchell. Only the latter survives, as the
older buildings could not be restructured
for new uses.*

Dallas Shops:
Dry-Goods Stores to Regional Malls

E. G. Hamilton, FAIA

Retail architecture in Dallas is similar to that in other
U.S. cities of the same approximate age and population
(100 to 150 years; half a million to two million people). The
sequence or evolution of retail development, as well as the
built products of each stage of evolution, follows a similar
pattern. Briefly, these have been the basic stages of growth:

1. In the early years the retail area was centrally located
adjacent to the largest concentration of population. That
area traditionally became the core of the city as it evolved.

2. Major department stores in this core began to develop
as a retail concept in the early part of the century. Service
retail stores followed the streetcar network out to the
newly created suburbs, forming nodes around the principal
suburban streetcar stops.

3. In response to a wider use of the automobile in the
1930s, strips of retail establishments began to fill in between
the nodes.

4. In the 1950s and early 1960s, there began a tremen-
dous suburban expansion. The large department stores
began to open branches in the suburbs, usually in centers
with small service retail stores at the intersections of major
suburban thoroughfares. The downtown core during those
years became a specialized business district, operating
essentially from 8:00 till 5:00 on weekdays.

5. Finally, the late 1960s and early 1970s brought the
large shopping malls, located where the new freeways
intersect and completely automobile oriented.

Dallas has an abundance of retail buildings representative
of each evolutionary stage. There are several buildings and
centers, however, that stand out as being unique to Dallas,
and that represent the development of the retail building
type in Dallas.

In considering the beginnings of retail business in Dallas,
we find that the department stores are significant historically. Sanger Harris (originally Sanger Brothers), Titche's,
and Neiman-Marcus — all large department stores now
owned by national chains — have been a part of Dallas
retailing since the City's earliest days.

The Sanger brothers first came to Dallas in 1872 with the
arrival of the Houston & Texas Central Railroad. They were
among a group of merchants, known appropriately as
Terminus Merchants, who followed the town-by-town
advance of the H & TC, setting up shops wherever the
railroad paused in its progress. When the railroad reached
Dallas, the Sanger brothers stayed. In 1873 they opened a
10,000-square-foot store at Elm, Austin, and Lamar. In 1902,
they began work on a new store at Main and Lamar. This
building, constructed in three phases between 1902 and
1912, is a clear example of the department-store style of the
day, with details strongly influenced by the Chicago School.
The building was designed by Lang & Witchell, a local
architectural firm no longer in practice. An additional point
that makes the 120,000-square-foot building significant is
that it has been recycled to house a successful urban junior
college, El Centro. The architect for this renovation was
The Oglesby Group.

The Titche-Goettinger Company opened its first store in 1902. In 1929 that store was replaced with a larger building of the department-store genre at Elm and St. Paul Streets; it was designed by Herbert Greene of Greene, LaRoche & Dahl (now Dahl, Braden & Chapman, Inc.). The building still stands and is another good example of the early type. The architects for this building, one of the oldest firms in Dallas, are responsible for much of the early department-store architecture in the city. Although Titche's has a number of suburban stores, the downtown building, expanded in 1955 to its present 470,000 square feet, is still considered its main store. The architects for the expansion were Thomas, Jameson & Merrill.

Neiman-Marcus is a nationally known specialty store, developed in large part by one of the greatest merchants of our time, Stanley Marcus. The original Neiman-Marcus store was built in 1914 at Main and Ervay Streets, and was designed by Herbert M. Greene Co. The first building, a red brick four-story structure, was expanded to Commerce Street in 1927, approximately doubling the original size. In 1928, a facade, which is still in place, was added. The building has undergone several other expansions over the years, including the addition of the new Man's Shop on Main Street in 1952 by DeWitt & Swank. The downtown Neiman-Marcus store, which presently has seven stories with more than 280,000 square feet, is still headquarters of the Neiman-Marcus operation, and it is here that Neiman's holds its annual "Fortnight," an event of international acclaim.

Another downtown building designed by Greene, LaRoche & Dahl that still stands (though in disuse) is the old Volk Building at 1810 Elm Street. It faces the street with an arched metal and glass canopy that spans almost the width of the structure. Although the building is small compared with the other department stores (only 52,000 square feet), the spaces inside are quite grand. The vaulted ceilings are high enough to allow a stock mezzanine around the perimeter of each floor. The Volk Building, completed in 1930, was the first in Dallas designed to be fully air conditioned. It seems to be a prime subject for a reuse study, and would provide space with character equalled by few other buildings in Downtown Dallas.

An early department store that should be mentioned here, even though it is not actually a "Dallas store," is the main Sears & Roebuck Catalogue Order and Retail Complex at 1409 Lamar. This giant complex was begun in 1906 as the first Sears & Roebuck Catalogue Order facility outside of Chicago. What is interesting about it is that it was built through a series of expansions throughout which a strong sense of unity was maintained simply through the use of a red and white horizontal banding on its skin. The building now contains three million square feet of floor space. The architect is unknown.

Titche-Goettinger 1929
Greene, LaRoche & Dahl
The photo dates from the opening of the 1929 store.

Upper left:
Neiman-Marcus, original store 1914
Herbert M. Greene Co.

Left:
Neiman-Marcus, addition and facade, 1928
Greene, LaRoche & Dahl
This is Neiman's Downtown as we know it today.

Sears Catalog & Retail Complex, detail

Left:
Detail, Neiman-Marcus

Highland Park Shopping Village 1931
Foshee & Cheek

Upper far right:
Sanger-Harris Downtown Store 1965
Thomas E. Stanley & Associates

Right:
Cullum & Boren Sporting Goods 1966
The Pierce-Lacey Partnership
1968 AIA Dallas Award
1966 TSA Award
Photo: Walter deLima Meyers
Challenging a primary retailing principle,
this highly successful downtown store
incorporates a landscaped courtyard with
storefront far from the street.

The Farmers Market
Taylor at S. Central Expressway
The Market, a popular Dallas institution
is being studied for urban design
improvements by the City Department of
Urban Planning. Farmers bring produce
from all parts of North Central Texas.
Drawing: Gary Skotnicki

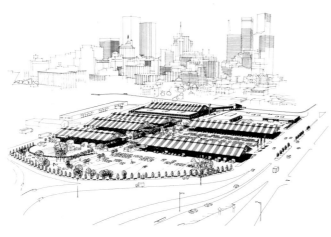

Department stores in Dallas began their move to the suburbs as early as 1941, when Sanger's opened a branch store in Highland Park Village. By the early 1960s almost all department-store development was taking place in suburban centers or malls. An exception that should be mentioned is the present downtown Sanger Harris. This 450,000-square-foot building at Akard and Pacific was built in 1965 at the peak of the flight to the suburbs. The store, designed by Thomas Stanley, is the headquarters for the entire Sanger Harris operation.

Shopping centers have proliferated in Dallas, as in most cities, in response to the new levels of mobility made possible by the widespread use of the automobile. Virtually everywhere that principal thoroughfares intersect in Dallas there is some sort of shopping center. However, it is only the off-street centers, planned or designed as a whole, that seem to be of any particular architectural interest.

Highland Park Shopping Village, at Preston Road and Mockingbird Lane, was the first planned, single-owner, off-street shopping center in the U. S. when it was begun in 1931. The complex, designed by Fooshee and Cheek, has 206,000 square feet of gross leasable area. The original "Moorish" architectural style, expressed in carved stone, cream stucco, and red tile, has been maintained throughout the years, and the center continues to thrive.

Another planned center of architectural interest is The Quadrangle (Pratt, Box & Henderson), at Routh Street and Cole Avenue. The project was built in 1965 with 48,000 square feet and then expanded in 1970 to 108,000 square feet. It is in the Oak Lawn area of Dallas, an area predominantly residential in scale, but one that has undergone some conversion in use. Many of the old houses are now specialty shops, galleries, professional offices, and restaurants. The Quadrangle has adopted this mixing of commercial uses as its own program. The project consists of a number of two-story stucco structures organized around a series of small courtyards, all residential in scale. In 1968 it won a Dallas Chapter AIA "Architecture '68" award, and later it was included in the Chapter's "Award 1970, Architecture of the Past Decade."

The Quadrangle
Pratt, Box, Henderson & Partners
1968 AIA Dallas Award
1970 AIA Dallas Award
The Courtyards of the Quadrangle

Photo credits:
Below, Steven Adams
Center, Leo B. Johnson
Lower right, Leo B. Johnson

Frank Parra Chevrolet 1974
ANPH
1975 AIA Dallas Award

Far right:
Treehouse 1975
The Pierce-Lacey Partnership;
Katzman/Kloke Design Consultants.
This renovation of a late 1950s
community shopping center was
architecturally successful.

Interior, Town East Mall 1971
Omniplan Architects Harrell + Hamilton
A regional mall with over a million square
feet of leasable area; the structural concept
of the central space is noteworthy.

In 1959, Big Town Mall, on Interstate Highway 20 at the intersection of Loop 12, opened with 600,000 square feet of gross leasable area as the first enclosed shopping mall in the southwest. The locating of this early mall adjacent to major freeways so that it could draw on the entire region as a market set the pattern for subsequent mall development. Big Town was designed by Tathum Quaid, a local architect. Besides being significant as the first mall in the Southwest, it is also significant as the first mall in the area to be completely recycled. The architects for the 1975 renovation were Copeland, Novak & Israel of New York. Big Town continues to be successful, even though there are newer malls not far away.

Old Town in the Village 1970
Envirodynamics
1972 TSA Award
1974 AIA Dallas Award
Although on a long, narrow site, Old Town is definitely not a strip center. Stores are clustered into squarish buildings that face parking streets on one side and pedestrian courtyards on the other.

Far left:
The Market at Old Vickery Square 1975
Manos & Muncey
Photo: Karl Stone

Left:
Olla Podrida 1972
Pratt, Box, Henderson & Partners,
Concept Architects; The Architects
Partnership, Design Architects.
1974 AIA Dallas Award
Photo: R. E. Tenney
An artsy-craftsy specialty shopping center
adapted from a series of metal storage
buildings. It is laid out in such a way that
one often must walk through the shops
themselves to get from place to place.
Interior construction materials are old
timbers and weathered boards.

Far left:
Willow Creek Shopping Village 1966
Ralph Kelman & Associates
1970 TSA Award
The east elevation clearly and charmingly
conveys the old-time values of "living over
the shop."

Carrollton Park Mall 1976
Burson, Hendricks & Walls
1977 AIA Dallas Award
The strip shopping center refined: Bold
rectangular solids create strong visual
identity for a building type that usually
lacks that quality.

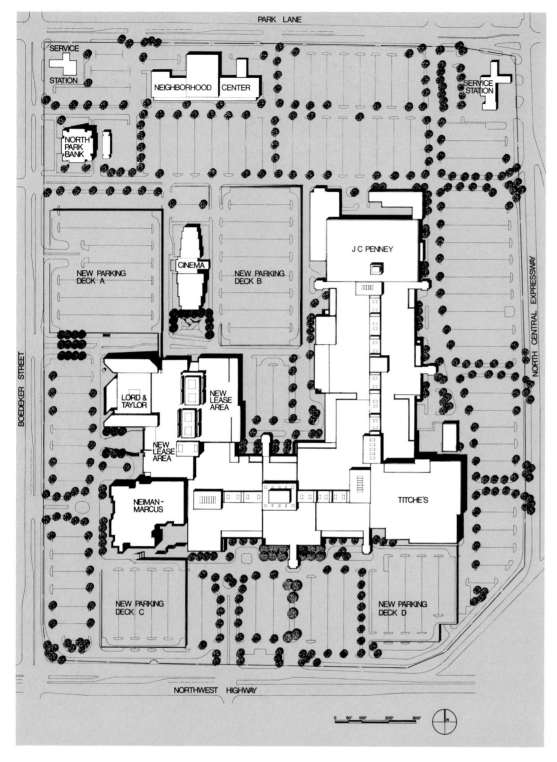

Several malls have been built in Dallas, mostly in the north part of the city, since Big Town was built. One that has gained national recognition for its popularity and productivity is NorthPark, at North Central Expressway (U.S. 75) and Loop 12 (Northwest Highway). NorthPark, owned by Raymond Nasher and designed by Omniplan Architects, was built in 1965, then expanded in 1975 to its current size of 1.6 million square feet of gross leasable area. It has won a number of design awards, including the AIA Decade Award.

These are not the only examples of interesting or significant retail architecture in Dallas. They are, however, a fairly good representation of architecturally worthy retail establishments in their varied forms.

NorthPark National Bank 1973
Omniplan Architects Harrell+Hamilton
Photo, interior: Mike Haynes
Photo, exterior: Dan Hatzenbuehler

Far left:
Interior, NorthPark
Photo: Ezra Stoller

Lord & Taylor
NorthPark Expansion 1975
Omniplan Architects Harrell+Hamilton
1975 AIA Dallas Award
1976 TSA Award
Changes in level on the site allowed for a
graceful introduction of parking decks.
Refer to plan on facing page.

Facing page:
Neiman-Marcus NorthPark 1965
Omniplan Architects Harrell+Hamilton
Eero Saarinen & Associates
South elevation NorthPark 1965
Omniplan Architects Harrell+Hamilton
1966 AIA Dallas Award
1967 TSA Award
1970 AIA Dallas Campbell & Tucker
Award

41

Garden Office Buildings — The Bottom Line

Jerrald L. Clement, AIA

Southwestern Life Insurance Co. 1964
George L. Dahl
1965 TSA Award

Right:
Great National Life Insurance Co. 1963
Grayson Gill

Dallas is a city of entrepreneurs, founded by the pioneer entrepreneur John Neely Bryan and built for the most part by businessmen who were firm believers in keeping the dirt flying. Garden offices as a building type, if not germinated by Dallas, at least have flowered in our city perhaps more so than elsewhere. Dallas has not been notable for great public architecture, although we now have our new City Hall and our Thanks-Giving Square. It is, rather, the architecture of commerce for which Dallas can be said to be notable — perhaps even unique. Garden office buildings are our own contribution to the architecture for the true twentieth-century patron, the real-estate entrepreneur.

The rationale for speculative office buildings is a positive cash flow on the bottom line of the financial sheet. For years, many architects tended to look with disdain (some still do) on the artistic challenge of the income-producing property. On the other hand, many real-estate developers tended to look with disdain (some still do) on architects as prima donnas to be used only for prestige, high-budget jobs. Architects were supposedly incapable of understanding the bottom line.

Today Dallas has a generation of architects who are not intimidated by the bottom line. Some have gotten into development themselves — with varying degrees of success, but at least they have become aware of the problems of the entrepreneur.

To some architects it may seem paradoxical to attempt to wed the art of architecture with the economic demands of commerce. Yet the essential elements of good design — concept, environmental harmony, functional appropriateness, crisp detailing, and form — can be applied within the discipline of a tight budget.

You may be saying, "OK, so the architecture of commerce is art for money. But what is a garden office building anyway?" A garden office building is not simply any low building leased as office space or used as a corporate headquarters; nor is it a moderately high building out in the suburbs with a fringe of wax-leaf ligustrum around the

parking lot. Rather, the typical garden office is one whose landscaping is integrated with the architecture. It is low, and the parking areas are relieved by greenery. Materials and detailing are less mechanistic and perhaps more humanistic than are found in a typical downtown office tower. It stands in what were formerly residential neighborhoods, either by itself or in clusters called garden office parks.

There are myriad variations on the theme. Dozens of so-called garden offices consist of a building of at best innocuous architecture, a parking lot, and not much else. The better examples of garden office architecture in Dallas consist of much more: architectural interest; at least a modicum of the natural (or contrived natural) environment; created exterior spaces in the case of groups of buildings; and interior spaces that have an interesting treatment of volumes. The opportunity to play with volumes, which is dear to the heart of all architects, is, however, somewhat limited in the speculative office building. The exception can be a single-user building such as a corporate or regional headquarters. The multiple-tenant building demands a fairly uniform ceiling height (8 feet 6 inches seems to be the norm) throughout the lease space. Lobbies, stairwells, and other public areas are the places to play the form and volume game. When the rest of the site is mostly parking lot, the building can be turned outside in, around an atrium filled with greenery. These were popular in some Dallas buildings long before the onset of the indoor plant craze.

Why would a developer go to the extra trouble of planting (or preserving) some trees in the parking lot, bringing some of the landscape inside, and building a structure of some architectural interest? Because it's good business, that's why! There is a growing trend in management circles to be more humanistic. The behavioral scientists have discovered that a pleasant, more individually scaled environment makes for happier and more productive employees. Many architects have been trying to sell that idea for years, and finally commerce is buying. Both for themselves and for their employees, many executives are as interested in the office environment as they are in their home environment; therefore, in scale and materials, many garden office buildings are almost homelike. Monumentality and hard materials are better suited to the downtown megaliths.

Planning a garden office park is largely a mathematical exercise to start with, based on zoning setback and density requirements, but based even more firmly on parking ratio. In Dallas the magic number is 1 to 300: one car to three hundred square feet of building. The economic feasibility of a project is rooted in a struggle among the parking ratio, the land cost, and the designer's determination to keep the world from becoming totally covered with asphalt (concrete is too expensive). Of course the rent is the other primary factor in the struggle. How it all comes out is a function of the architect's ingenuity in juggling the building geometry to get the highest ratio of building to land and the highest ratio of net leasable area to gross area (efficiency). If he's lucky he can throw in a bit of landscaping and some interesting architecture. To be successful in juggling these elements is to be successful in creating good garden office projects.

In the 1950s, Dallas garden office buildings were hardly deserving of the name. It was a time when contemporary architecture was just beginning to win in the struggle with the Beaux Arts neoclassical tradition. You remember: Banks were neoclassical; Savings and Loans and Insurance Companies were Georgian with little white cupolas on top. Much of the contemporary style of that time was cosmetic only. Landscaping consisted of a St. Augustine lawn, two mimosa trees, and abelia to hide the foundation.

In the early 1960s, the garden office came into its own in Dallas, largely owing to an aggressive real-estate market. There were more opportunities for architects to design commercial projects, and indeed more opportunities for architects to build buildings for themselves.

Dr Pepper National Headquarters
Executive Office Expansion 1974
Ralph Kelman & Associates
The glass block walls of the addition extend diagonally from the stepped wings of the original building.

First Federal Savings & Loan 1974
The Pierce-Lacey Partnership
1975 AIA Dallas Award
The transformation of the old Neiman-Marcus store in Preston Center (above) was complete. Of special interest is the glass-enclosed garden in the lobby.

Right:
Lemmon Park North 1971
Envirodynamics

Below right:
One Lemmon Park East 1964
Woodward, Cape & Associates
1966 AIA Dallas Award
1966 TSA Award

Lemmon Park West 1971
Envirodynamics

The Lemmon Park area in near North Dallas just west of Central Expressway was spawned by an architectural firm who built first for their own needs because there was nothing appropriate available. One thing led to another, one building led to another, and a garden office park was born. The area was, in 1964, a residential area that had seen better days. Office zoning in the neighborhood made possible a transition to commercial use. The land was dotted with seventy-year-old post oaks, a rarity in this formerly prairie country. Conventional procedures for developing real estate would have sent the venerable oak trees toppling before the bulldozers, but the architects had the foresight and salesmanship to convince a lender that a small office building of white stucco and redwood surrounded by "growies" was a good investment. As more lots became available, additional buildings of increasing size were built.

One Lemmon Park East, one of the first low buildings in Dallas to be built on stilts over parking space, was carefully fitted around the existing trees. The center courtyard originally contained a number of marvelous old post oaks. Unfortunately, this variety of tree can suddenly turn up its toes for no apparent reason, and many of the original trees have died. This building complex (Lemmon Park East, One through Four) was the recipient in 1966 of both a Dallas Design Award and a TSA award. (At the time, it was unusual for income-producing properties to be so honored. Today, a majority of Dallas Design Awards are for commercial projects.) Lemmon Park East exemplifies another unique aspect of this building type — the piece-meal acquisition of land. The sites were assembled from small lots. Sitting cheek by jowl with the office buildings is a collector of junque who is still holding out.

Located on another block and fronting on McKinney is Lemmon Park West, another segment of this white stucco complex. In addition to a series of turrets it has Ventwood sunscreens, a characteristic of the Lemmon Park buildings as well as of other garden office buildings of the era. (The architects were concerned about the cost of cooling ten years before the energy crisis.) A bridge over a public alley connects the two wings of the building. Here again, several of the old oaks have died and something of the original character has been lost. Lemmon Park West houses the Southwest Regional Headquarters of Xerox. Their corporate decision to move into a two-story North Dallas garden building was a shocker in the real-estate circles of 1967.

Taken all together, although it was not necessarily the first of the breed, the Lemmon Park garden-office complex is something of a prototype for garden-office buildings in Dallas. It shows how seven different buildings involving varying programs and radically different site geometries can be tied together by using a dominant material throughout — in this case, white stucco.

In the same part of town (Oak Lawn) there are a number of interesting, small garden office buildings, many built by architects for their own use or as investments. These include the buildings at 2710 Oak Lawn (the garden is on the inside) and across the street at 2727 Oak Lawn. The latter is notable less for the gardens than for a certain elegance in the proportions of the "Chicago style" windows and exposed steel frame with Mexican brick infill panels. Each represents two poles of architectural expression: one very residential in scale, materials, and details; the other almost "Miesian." Residential scale is axiomatic for many of the garden office buildings of the 1960s. The whole idea was to create an office home. This sort of artsy-craftsy approach can be seen at 2919 Welborn, where, again, the garden court is inside the building. (To see the building, one must park, since it is set back from the street behind what was probably the original retaining wall.) There are many other examples in the Oak Lawn area, the small office buildings having become as much a part of the character of the neighborhood as the substantial old homes, oaks, and cedar elms. As for the ticky-tacky commercial development, both old and new, along Oak Lawn and Lemmon, the less said the better.

Dallas is essentially a city of north-south axes; the action outside of downtown has primarily been bounded by Central Expressway on the east, Stemmons Freeway on the west, and Oak Lawn Avenue on the south. In its relentless growth, Dallas, like an astonishing number of other cities, has pushed to the north.

Above:
Bruton Park, 8700 N. Stemmons 1972
Neuhaus + Taylor
1973 AIA Dallas Award
Photo: Richard Payne

Upper right:
Chilton Corporation 1965
The Pierce-Lacey Partnership

Right:
Royal National Bank 1969
Harwood K. Smith & Partners
1969 TSA Award

Elmbrook Gardens 1972
Travers-Johnston, Portland, Oregon
Exterior, above; Interior, right

As the affluent moved north to live, commercial enterprises followed; and in their wake, office developments sprang up along the principal north-south arteries. Garden office buildings in the move northward lost something of their residential qualities, grew larger, and lost the natural character of the oak groves of near North Dallas. The garden environments had to be created. Three-inch-caliper trees and monkey grass take a while to resemble the architect's rendering. There are a number of interesting office projects along both Central Expressway and Stemmons Freeway. However, the character of the garden office as a distinctive type has become rather blurred. Some, like the RCA regional headquarters building at 8700 N. Stemmons, are fairly monumental; but in the case of the RCA building the interior court does retain the feeling of a garden. There is an unfortunate plethora of low high-rise or high low-rise office buildings along Stemmons that are in the "plunked down in a parking lot" style. An interesting exception is the Elmbrook Gardens building, with one of the nicer atrium spaces in Dallas.

On Central Expressway, the right-hand corridor on the Dallas city map, is Meadow Park Central, a good example of a garden office. The axial courtyard contains some of the nicer commercial landscaping in town; the use of water is especially effective. When the project was built (1969) it took considerable courage on the part of the developer to devote a substantial part of the budget to a man-made landscape. The investment seems to have paid off, for the occupancy rate is high. And that's the whole point of garden-office design, remember? To see this one, take the Meadow Road exit off North Central Expressway.

You might, on the way out, take the Walnut Hill Lane exit and go east. You will come to Woodhill, a development that has done a good job of preserving the original grove of oaks. The reverence for trees constantly alluded to here reflects something of the Dallas ecology: mostly raw prairie bisected at intervals by tree-lined creek bottoms. Many of the original tree-lined creeks and lowland groves have been lost; those that remain are a precious commodity with great value on the bottom line of the financial sheet as well as on the ecological ledger. The Woodhill complex, by the way, has some interesting architecture and graphics as well as trees.

The decade of the 1970s saw the completion of an east-west corridor bisecting the north-south axis. Lyndon B. Johnson Freeway generated a modest boom of real estate speculation and commercial development, much of which is typical urban sprawl. There are, however, some garden office developments. The Registry on LBJ just east of Preston Road is one of the better examples. The building forms and green spaces are the principal interest. Metro Square, off LBJ near Josey Lane is another development representative of the garden office concept. One Metro Square is an X-shaped building with a man-made lagoon in front and one of the more impressive architectural logos in town. Two Metro Square has a brook meandering through the lobbies and courtyards. All of the garden effect had to be created on this otherwise featureless site.

Park Central, near the intersection of Central Expressway and LBJ, is not a garden office complex at all, but Park Central Tower has a seven-story semi-atrium that is interesting, although it looks unfinished. The scale of this development makes it something of an out-of-town downtown, but there still remains considerable undeveloped land, and the trees and terrain are suitable for green spaces that could be integrated with the architecture. Let us hope the developer is listening.

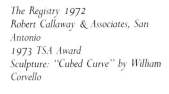

The Registry 1972
Robert Callaway & Associates, San Antonio
1973 TSA Award
Sculpture: "Cubed Curve" by William Corvello

Above:
View of Park Central II, 1972 (left) and III, 1975
John Portman, Atlanta (I & II);
Jarvis Putty Jarvis (III).
In this case, the "garden" encompasses nearly one square mile.

Left:
Heritage Square Office Park 1977
Pratt, Box, Henderson & Partners
Concrete parts were precast on the job site.

Woodhill Medical Park 1975
Olds-Udstuen-Thompson

Above:
Redman Plaza 1972
Ralph Kelman & Associates
1973 TSA Award
1974 AIA Dallas Award

Upper right:
Safeco Insurance Co. 1977
Iconoplex

Middle right:
Office building for The Richards Group
1976
Fisher & Spillman
1976 TSA Award
Photo: Craig D. Blackmon

Of course, not all the garden offices are in Oak Lawn or on the principal automobile corridors. For example, Redman Plaza at 2550 Walnut Hill Lane is an outstanding project with some very nice landscaping. Nor is the list of buildings mentioned here at all complete. A sprawling city like Dallas has many jewels in its crown, along with its full share of thorns. If, like me, you're an aficionado of a particular building type, you'll find it fun to get in your car and explore. And exploring Dallas does require a car (cab mileage could be astronomical), for Big D, like L.A., is a creature of the automobile. The garden office building is also a creature of the automobile: The landscaping and screening of parking areas inherent in successful garden-office design reflects the fact that cars, while some may be handsome enough individually, are messy in the aggregate.

Many people, for many reasons, like to work close to where they live. If we architects do our job well, we can accommodate that preference and do it in a way that achieves harmony, continuity, and a pleasing transition from office to home sweet home.

Sumet-Bernet Sound Studio 1970
Craycroft-Lacy & Partners
1971 TSA Award
Photo: Jess Alford

The Multistory Office Building

Harwood K. Smith, AIA

The history of the multistory office building in Dallas and its suburban areas is a history of constant and continuing change — in location, size, environment, client, economics, codes, ordinances, life style, industrial innovation and product improvement, and labor change. The following pages touch upon those changes, upon influences on the structures, and the architectural response.

By 1908, Dallas had one fifteen-story building, the Praetorian Building. In 1913 the Gothic-influenced Busch Building was constructed; it was sixteen stories high. The Magnolia Building, completed in 1921, rose to thirty-three stories and remained Dallas's tallest building for twenty years. In the period from 1908 to 1940, twenty-two multistory office buildings were erected, all in the Central Business District (CBD).

By 1960, the number had increased to forty buildings; three were more than forty stories high. Dallas now has nearly two hundred multistory office buildings, three of them more than fifty stories high.

Magnolia Building 1921
Alfred C. Bossom, New York & London
Photo: Doug Tomlinson
The revolving flying red horse was a landmark to travelers for years. Two signs were placed back-to-back so that no one could call Dallas a one-horse town. This building is now on the National Register of Historic Places.

Left:
Photo: Squire Haskins

49

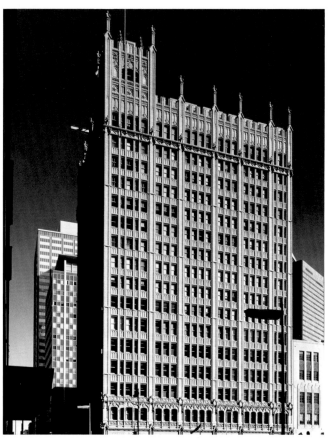

In 1930, twenty of the tall buildings were in the CBD and two were in the suburbs. By 1960, forty-seven of the buildings were in the CBD, and those in the suburbs had increased to twenty. Today there are fifty-two in the CBD, but over a hundred and thirty in the suburbs

Translating this into leasable area, in 1970 the CBD had 10.5 million square feet of office space and the suburbs had 4 million. By 1977, however, the leasable area in the CBD had increased by less than forty percent, whereas that in the suburbs had more than tripled, surpassing the CBD leasable space by 700,000 square feet.

The Praetorian building of 1908 contained 155,000 square feet. The net leasable floor space of the Busch Building (now the United National Bank Building, refurbished and thriving) is 150,000 square feet; that of the Magnolia Building (now called the Mobil Building, and recently given to the City of Dallas) is 176,750 square feet. The Republic National Bank Building, erected in 1954, contains 876,000 square feet. Continuing the trend of taller and bigger, a fifty-two story structure built in 1965 had 1.6 million square feet in it, and a fifty-six-story building erected in 1974 had 1.8 million square feet. All of those buildings were in the Central Business District.

While this was going on, the buildings in the suburbs were increasing in numbers and also in volume and floor space. In 1975 a twenty-one-story building, Park Central, was constructed on North Central Expressway; it contained 550,000 square feet. In general, the suburban buildings have been smaller than those in the CBD.

Before 1950, most buildings were built for and by institutions, banks, insurance companies, and the like. Beginning in the late 1940s and early 1950s, the developer-owned structures began to emerge. Since that time, the developer and institutions have shared about equally in the Central City developments. In the suburbs, starting about the mid-1960s, it was the apartment and warehouse developer who began to get involved in multistory buildings.

It was natural for the developers to continue working where they had always worked — out of downtown. They could start small on land they understood and with which they felt at home. They could grow as their knowledge and experience grew. They could grow with the new market place created by the people sprawl. These developer clients had an additional asset: They knew the institutions and the people in them. The ones who made loans also knew how to make workable *pro formas*; in short, they knew how to get the needed money. By 1972, one of this group had moved downtown to erect one of Dallas's largest buildings. It is worth noting that three of the largest developers in the U.S.A. — Trammel Crow, John Eulich, and J.L. Williams — are in Dallas.

One Brookhollow Plaza 1969
Paul M. Rudolph, New York, and
Harwood K. Smith & Partners, Joint
Venture Architects.
Photo: Doug Tomlinson
This is the first and, so far, the only total
precast concrete multistory building in the
Southwest.

After World War II, the automobile took over. To accommodate it, the highway systems, both state and federal, spread like a web. People moved to the suburbs in droves and the office buildings followed the work force, lining up along the corridors.

The Stemmons corridor now has fifty-one buildings with 5.7 million square feet of leasable space. The LBJ corridor has thirty-two buildings, with 3.1 million square feet; North Central Expressway has twenty-six buildings, with 2.3 million square feet; and the Oak Lawn-Turtle Creek corridor has twenty-four buildings, with 1.25 million leasable square feet.

In the Central Business District, the cost of real estate has constantly increased. By and large, institutions erect buildings to serve their business functions and also to project an image, and they will stretch for height to achieve that image. But when the price per square foot of downtown real estate goes from ten dollars to a hundred dollars, another factor comes to bear. As the cost of land goes up, the buildings, of necessity, go up. Each square foot of ground must carry more building to pay for it.

In the suburbs the land prices were, originally, quite reasonable. But as zoning falsely raised the price of land, and as syndicators came in and parlayed the game out of reason, the prices skyrocketed. In fact, in the past few years the cost of property has increased proportionately faster in the suburbs than in the CBD. Suburban buildings, therefore, have also been forced to go higher, and now there is a twenty-one-story building on the LBJ corridor.

Up to and through World War II, the business community was connected quite firmly to the Central Business District. After the War, however, as a result of the changing times, the climate changed in the business community. Life, even working life, became more relaxed and people wanted more relaxed surroundings. They began moving from the CBD to the suburbs, where land was cheap and plentiful, where the working atmosphere was amiable, and where they could be aware of the landscape. They discovered "environment" as if it had never existed before.

A new competitiveness prompted developers to reevaluate the Central Business District. They began to bring open landscaping inside their buildings and to pay attention to natural landscaping outside. The City, also becoming more conscious of the downtown environment, began providing green spaces, parks, underground service tunnels, and parking structures. The center of town is becoming more and more attractive, so that one can choose a pleasant place to work, either downtown or farther out, according to what his business requirements are and what style of working life suits him best.

Mary Kay Office Building 1978
Foster + Meier

Sixty-Sixty Place 1972
Harwood K. Smith & Partners
1973 TSA Award
1972 AIA Dallas Award
The award-winning restaurant building
shares its site with an office tower and a
hotel.

53

While Dallas office buildings were going through the evolution from simple structures to large, fifty-story complexes, the products, the systems, and their components were undergoing comparable changes. The frame in the early building was a simple concrete structure. The electrical and mechanical system was minimal and also rather simple. As the client's requirements became more complicated, special systems were developed to serve them. All the elements from electrical to aesthetic underwent great changes. Industry applied its productivity and genius: Concrete and steel were strengthened; engineering designs were changed and improved; materials became a great deal lighter. The location of special structural members was changed to cope more efficiently with wind loads and floor loads as the buildings became taller. Electrical and mechanical systems were totally revolutionized and continue to improve and change. The requirements of a fifty-story building with 1.5 million square feet are vastly different from those of a fifteen-story building with 150,000 square feet.

The people-mover requirements are vastly different. The architect/engineer introduced such devices as escalators and double-decked elevators — the latter occupying less space but meeting peak demands.

A heightened interest in interior and exterior landscaping and plants opened up a whole new field: the study of plant life and the artificial light required to maintain growth.

Great aesthetic changes began to appear with the introduction of the glass curtain wall with its low cost, light weight, quickness and ease of erection, and the visibility it provides. The exteriors of the older buildings were mostly brick, which served well as long as the buildings were fairly low. But as the buildings became taller, they became heavier and harder to erect. Those problems, coupled with a scarcity of good masons, forced the architect and industry to find a more efficient way to handle brick. They developed sections of brick that could be assembled at ground level and raised in large units. Now brick is returning to the office tower.

In the early buildings all interior partitions were of plaster. But the industry improved sheetrock material, its connections, and it components, and now plaster is almost nonexistent.

Finished flooring in the older buildings was concrete, or wood on concrete. Through the years, floors have gone through many vogues: asphalt tile, rubber tile, terrazzo. Today, office buildings have mostly carpeted floors, and special materials such as granite, brick, and terra cotta in the lobby and exterior areas.

Simplicity and ease of installation have been the goals in designing multistory office buildings. Now easily constructed, easily cleaned, and well-detailed metal components, door frames, fire stairways, slab doors, lay-in ceilings, rubber base moulding — all of these are in common use.

The office buildings that architects have designed in Dallas have changed as requirements and technology have changed — in size, in sophistication, and in aesthetics. Most of the early multistory buildings in the area were designed by small architectural firms. Budgets were tight. For the most part the engineering was unsophisticated and the aesthetic involvement was minimal, hence also the result. The buildings were generally of structural concrete with brick exteriors and wooden double-hung windows. Buildings had a single client and a single purpose. This changed as the affluence of the society changed.

In 1943 the thirty-three-story Mercantile Bank was erected as a bank and office building. Built of a concrete frame with a brick and masonry exterior, it contained a mechanical system that could completely control the environment.

In 1954, the forty-story Republic National Bank was built. The exterior is lightweight embossed aluminum. Interior amenities include escalators, year-round air conditioning, and high-speed elevators.

Some clients require more on their property than one building devoted exclusively to offices. In 1959 Dallas got its first cluster of diversified buildings, the Southland Center. It contains a forty-two-story office building, a Sheraton Hotel, a shopping mall, restaurants, clubs, and a large underground parking garage. The structure is steel; the exterior is a curtain wall and precast masonry.

In 1968, the Main Place project was developed. It, also, was designed as a large complex with underground parking, underground pedestrianways, shopping plazas, a fountain plaza, a bank, an office building, and a club. Hotels and additional office buildings are to be erected in the future. The structure's exterior is of cast-in-place concrete and riverbed granite with a sandblasted surface applied under a French patent called "arbeton."

In 1972, a forty-story office tower was erected at 2001 Bryan. The exterior of the building is completely curtain walled, and it has a sophisticated steel structure and a nicely appointed lobby. The building, which has a particularly handsome exterior, is complemented by trees, sculpture, and masonry paving in a serpentine design.

Left:
Republic National Bank Building (right)
1954
Harrison & Abramowitz, New York;
Gill and Harrell, Associated Architects.
Republic Bank Tower, 1964
Omniplan Architects Harrell + Hamilton

Far left:
2001 Bryan Tower 1972
Neuhaus + Taylor, Houston

Above & left:
One Main Place 1968
Skidmore, Owings & Merrill, New York,
and Harwood K. Smith & Partners,
Associated Architects.
1970 AIA Dallas Award
Photo above: Hank Tenny

Above:
First National Bank Building 1964
George L. Dahl and Thomas E. Stanley,
Joint Venture Architects

Far right:
Oak Cliff Bank & Trust Co. 1965
Harwood K. Smith & Partners
Photo: John Rogers

Right:
First International Building 1975
Harwood K. Smith & Partners;
Hellmuth, Obata & Kassabaum, St. Louis,
Associated Architects.
1975 TSA Award
Photo: Barbara Martin

First International Building
Lobby interior
Photo: Hedrich-Blessing

In 1974, the First International Building, the second stage of the First National Bank complex, was erected. This fifty-six-story building contains 1.8 million square feet, has a reflective glass exterior wall, structural steel frame, tunnels connecting it with First National Bank and Main Place, granite paving, lobbies, an exterior garden, and a drive-through bank. It includes double-deck elevators, special flooring systems to accommodate all the requirements of the present-day office building, and the latest in security controls.

The buildings described above are all in the Central Business District. While those buildings were being built downtown, comparable but smaller complexes were being built in the suburbs. To name a few: Exchange Park was erected in 1955; Stemmons Towers in 1962; Oak Cliff Bank in 1965; the Zale Corporation headquarters in 1970; Campbell Centre in 1972; One Energy Square in 1974; Park Central in 1975.

Stemmons Towers 1962 - 1967
Harold A. Berry

Lower Left:
Zale Corporation Headquarters Building
1970
Harwood K. Smith & Partners

Below:
Campbell Centre
Phase One: Neuhaus + Taylor 1972
Phase Two: Harwood K. Smith
& Partners 1977

57

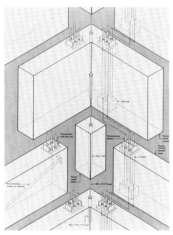

Citizens Bank and Office Tower 1974
Omniplan Architects Harrell + Hamilton
1975 AIA Dallas Award
1976 TSA Award
Photo: Dan Hatzenbuehler
Detail: Datum Structures Engineering
Precast concrete spandrel beams, 105 feet
long, span from corner to corner and
support the floor slabs, leaving the interior
column-free. This structural innovation
produced architectural clarity and leasing
advantages.

Far left:
Photo: Hedrich-Blessing

Left:
National Chemsearch Corporation 1974
Harwood K. Smith & Partners
Photo: John Rogers

Southland Corporation Headquarters
1971
Fisher & Spillman
1973 AIA Dallas Award
1973 AIA Dallas Campbell & Tucker
Award

The architectural/engineering offices that have produced those buildings have been many and varied. Most of the earlier structures were designed by small firms of ten men or less. As the schemes became larger and more complicated, it became necessary for firms — usually large ones, and often from distant parts of the country — to come together in joint ventures or consortiums. This appears to be an established pattern that will continue with the trend away from the single office tower toward the larger, more complex multiple-use project.

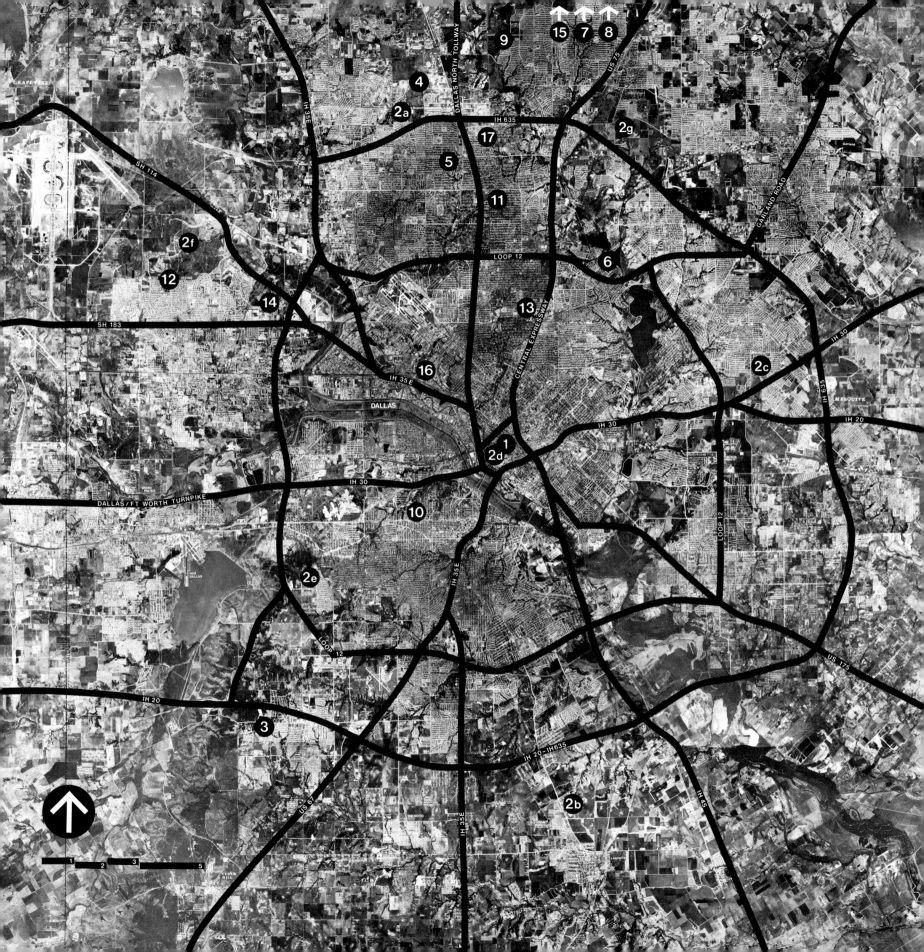

Chapter 4
Education

Dallas — The Halls of Learning

Donald E. Jarvis, FAIA

Dallas's existing educational architecture reflects many of the facets of Dallas itself — its newness, its cultural maturity, its citizen awareness and drive. Designing schools for Dallas today offers the architects, the educators, and the public many challenges that, if successfully met, could enrich the lives of tomorrow's citizens in far more significant ways than has the educational architecture of the past.

By far the largest school district in the Dallas area is the Dallas Independent School District, with over 200 buildings and more than 150,000 students. One of its two earliest buildings, the Cumberland Hill School, constructed in 1888, still stands in the Central Business District. It was operated as a school until the late 1960s. Early in the 1970s it was purchased by Southeastern Drilling Co. and converted into their corporate offices. The sensitive restoration and remodeling won its architects, Burson, Hendricks & Associates a design award.

From the time the Cumberland School was built until World War II, there was very little change in Dallas school design. Symmetrical, imposing, monumental facades incorporated the inevitable exterior stairs leading up about half a flight to the main floor. Typically, half a flight down were the lunchroom, toilets, and boiler room. On the main floor was the auditorium; and high-ceilinged classrooms filled out the rest of the main floor and one above it. About the only innovation that took place in fifty years of school design was the change from load-bearing masonry with timber floor-framing to more fire-resistive steel and concrete construction. Heating was universally by steam radiators, and lighting was almost nonexistent.

Most of the DISD's growth took place after World War II to accommodate the baby boom and the increase in immigrating population. The number of buildings in the District increased from 49 in 1945 to 203 in 1975.

Architecturally, the post-war era evidenced the worst and best characteristics of explosive growth and bigness. For more than a decade, the design and construction of this great number of buildings was coordinated by a single team of architects who saw to it that a fixed set of DISD standards was

adhered to. As a result, in the great majority of Dallas schools, one can find typical-size classrooms having typical cabinets in each corner and outfitted with typical chalkboards. The buildings were well constructed and are extremely well maintained, but they are stereotyped in design. Only occasionally did the buildings of that era show creativity or innovation. Some of the better ones are the Hexter Elementary School on Waterview, the Dealey Elementary School on Royal Lane, the Hotchkiss Elementary School on Town North Drive, and the Comstock Junior High School on Hodde Street.

During the growth period efforts were concentrated on putting a roof over the children's heads at the lowest cost per child. But there was little coordination between DISD planning and City of Dallas planning. Some schools are poorly located in relation to City growth and in relation to street patterns. In some instances, the campuses are too small.

In the mid-1960s there was a significant change in the planning procedures for the DISD. The Dallas Chapter of the American Institute of Architects became heavily involved in a cooperative effort to upgrade the District's schools. A cooperative attitude persists, and through a standing committee of the AIA there is an opportunity for the DISD Board of Trustees, the Administration, and architects to freely exchange ideas and constructive comments.

Far right:
Cumberland Hill School c. 1888
Restoration 1971: Burson, Hendricks & Associates
1971 TSA Award
1971 AIA Dallas Award

Hotchkiss Elementary School 1962
Fisher & Jarvis

It is too early to assess the school architecture of the current era. One thing is certain: few projects follow the tradition of erecting new buildings on virgin land. With the thought of learning what are the greatest needs, architects and the DISD are soliciting the opinions of citizens for the programming stages. Such an approach has its drawbacks. It is difficult to keep logical long-range education goals in sight in the face of what are often parochial, contradictory community pressures.

The challenge facing Dallas architects is not only to design good school buildings, but also to exercise diplomacy and leadership in the community. To the extent that they succeed, their efforts will favorably affect the children of Dallas and therefore the City as a whole.

Dallas is ringed with thirteen suburban school districts. Most are in the same county, and one — the Highland Park Independent School District — is surrounded by the DISD. In general, most of the growth in those districts has taken place since 1960. In this period, Garland, Mesquite, Irving, and Richardson, for example, have more than tripled in size.

In most suburban districts the new residents insist that taxes be kept low (low taxes are one reason they move to the suburbs). This tends to make construction budgets tight and allows for little beyond bare necessities. Yet some districts have capitalized on their smallness and lack of stereotyped standards to innovate. Plano and Duncanville, for example, early moved into team teaching, and they, like several other districts, included air-conditioning in their standards for new schools. Plano has divided its high schools, separating the 9th and 10th grades from the 11th and 12th grades, which offer a number of career-oriented programs.

Rosemont Elementary School 1973
Harold E. Prinz

Far left:
E.D. Walker Middle School 1972
Dales Y. Foster

Before the new procedures could result in many buildings, a desegregation lawsuit brought construction to a virtual halt. Nevertheless, a large new facility, Skyline High School, had already been planned, so it was completed. With the active involvement of the business community, Skyline's pro-grammed emphasis on vocational and technical training was modified. The result was a career-centered curriculum that became a great pioneering effort for the DISD. Skyline has won national acclaim for its outstanding educational impact (although not, so far, for its architecture). Also completed in this period was the E. D. Walker Middle School on Nuestra Drive; it was Dallas's first open-plan school. Although con-struction of new buildings had ceased, a large-scale program for air-conditioning all the schools in the District was begun.

For more than five years, most new construction was stalled. But in that period an entirely new set of problems arose that presented an opportunity for experimentation. Popu-lation shifts became dramatic. Schools in several areas of the District were well below capacity, partly because the birthrate had declined, partly because many whites, in frus-tration over uncertainties, had moved to the suburbs. Yet other areas of the DISD experienced extreme overcrowding. A large number of portable and demountable structures were produced, from the size of a classroom to that of a gymnasium and a full elementary school. One of the better such structures is the B. F. Darrell School on South Lancaster Road. A pilot project for recycling an old school into a team-teaching, open-plan, carpeted facility was undertaken with consider-able success. This project, the Rosemont School on North Montclair Avenue, was studied for its promise of what could be done in older areas with older buildings.

Leading Dallas citizens were painfully aware that Dallas's heritage of a strong public school system could be lost unless community-wide action and support could be mustered. A plan to settle the desegregation suit was evolved by a community organization, the Dallas Alliance. Strong sup-port was generated and an $80-million Bond Program was passed that included a large number of renovation projects and the creation of a new building type — the magnet school — using Skyline's career-emphasis programs as a pattern.

Plano Senior High School 1976
Jarvis Putty Jarvis
Photo: John Rogers

Sam Houston Jr. High School 1976
Grogan & Scoggins, Irving
1977 AIA Dallas Award

Duncanville High School 1965
Jarvis Putty Jarvis
1970 AIA Dallas Award
Photo: William J. Davis

Jackson Elementary School 1975
Corgan Associates
Photo: Justin Rollins

Several schools in the suburban districts have received design awards and citations: Duncanville High School in Duncanville; Prestonwood Elementary School in Richardson; and Sigler and Jackson Elementary Schools in Plano. Other fine schools have been built in Carrollton-Farmers Branch (designed by John R. Thompson & Associates), and in Mesquite and Garland (designed by Wright-Rich & Associates).

The suburban school districts are still growing — some at an astounding pace. There is a danger that in the haste of constructing, thoughtful designing and sound planning will fall by the way. Architects for those districts may again have to call upon their leadership skills to encourage the community to continue emphasizing good architecture.

Prestonwood Elementary School 1972
Jarvis Putty Jarvis

The number of students attending private school in the Dallas area is very small compared with that attending public schools. Yet a few established private schools have had a greater impact architecturally than their enrollments would suggest.

St. Mark's School, on Preston Road, probably has the most outstanding campus. Its recent buildings are excellent, particularly the H. Ben Decherd Center for arts and drama, and the library (designed by Ford, Powell & Carson of San Antonio). The Lamplighter School on Inwood Road (Ford, Powell & Carson) also provides a fine environment for its young students. The Hockaday School became a coherent campus built all at one time when it relocated to its present site on Welch Road.

These and several others are worthy of attention, since they have placed a premium on the effects that good design can have on education. A number of new private schools were created during the unsettled times of the DISD desegregation suit. Many occupy existing facilities such as churches, and there are few projects of architectural significance among them.

St. Mark's School of Texas
Top right:
H. Ben Decherd Center for
Performing Arts 1974
The Oglesby Group
1975 AIA Dallas Award
Photo: John Rogers
Above:
Science & Mathematics
Quadrangle 1961
O'Neil Ford, S. B. Zisman,
Duane Landry, Associated Architects

Far left:
Greenhill School Preschool Facility 1974
The Oglesby Group
1975 AIA Dallas Award
Photo: John Rogers

Left:
The Hockaday School 1963
Harwood K. Smith & Partners

Right:
Southern Methodist University
Underwood Law Library 1970
Thomas, Booziotis & Associates
Harper & Kemp Consulting Architects
Photo: Wayne Thom

Upper far right:
Southern Methodist University
Dallas Hall 1915
Shepley, Rutan & Coolidge, Boston
Restoration 1970: The Pierce-Lacey
Partnership

Center far right:
Southern Methodist University
Fondren Library Extension 1963 (right)
Harper & Kemp
Science Information Center 1961 (left)
O'Neil Ford and A. B. Swank
Photo: Bill Cox

Lower far right:
Southern Methodist University
View from Dallas Hall looking
south on Bishop Blvd.
Photo: Kenneth Konlande

University of Dallas
Campanile 1968
O'Neil Ford and Duane Landry,
Associated Architects

Right:
University of Dallas
Haggar University Center 1976
Ford, Powell & Carson; and
Duane Landry, Associated Architects
1977 AIA Dallas Award

Facilities for higher education have followed a pattern
of growth similar to that of the schools in Dallas, only a few
years later in the cycle.

Through World War II, the principal institution of
higher learning in the Dallas area was Southern Methodist
University. There were also public colleges available in Denton, 30 miles away, and a public junior college in Arlington,
15 miles away. The SMU campus was established in 1915
with the building of Dallas Hall, a well proportioned, domed
structure, neoclassic in style but Georgian in materials. The
Georgian prevailed, and was the style adhered to throughout
the execution of the rigid campus plan. For all the visual continuity created by such a plan, it also engendered stereotyped
design, and few buildings of merit followed the first one.
Distinguished exceptions are the Science Information Center,
built in 1961, the Fondren Library Extension added in 1963,
and the more recent Underwood Law Library.

The University of Dallas, a Roman Catholic institution,
is situated on a beautiful hillside in Irving. The campus, which
has some early, unexceptional buildings, has been dramatically improved by site development and by the addition of
a graceful red brick campanile, as well as other good-looking
structures such as the Union Building. Ford, Powell & Carson
designed the more recent additions.

Richland College 1972
The Oglesby Group; Oglesby, Wiley
Halford; and The Perkins & Will
Partnership, Chicago, Associated Architects
1973 AIA Dallas Award
Photo: John Rogers

With the creation of the Dallas County Community College District in the early 1960s, a breath of fresh air came to educational architecture in Dallas. An enlightened Board of Trustees and a strong Administrator seized the opportunity to create a countywide system comprising a downtown college and six suburban colleges. They placed a high priority on design and on careful programming of needs. The results are impressive and stand as an example to all educational entities of how to create buildings for learning. All campuses are completed or nearing completion, and every one that is completed has received design awards and has been published widely.

El Centro College 1967
The Oglesby Group; Oglesby, Wiley,
Halford
1966 TSA Award
1970 AIA Dallas Award
Photo: John Rogers

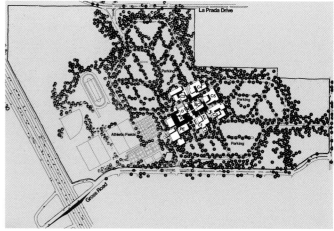

Right:
El Centro College
Restoration 1967: The Oglesby Group;
Oglesby, Wiley, Halford
Originally Sanger Bros. Department Store
1910, Lang & Witchell.
Photo: John Rogers

Eastfield College 1970
Harwood K. Smith & Partners;
and Ernest J. Kump Associates, Palo Alto,
Associated Architects
1971 TSA Award
1971 AIA Dallas Award
1971 Campbell & Tucker Award
Photo: John Rogers

Upper right:
Eastfield College
Site Plan

Mountainview College 1970
Omniplan Architects Harrell + Hamilton;
and Chan/Rader, San Francisco,
Associated Architects
1971 AIA Dallas Award
1971 TSA Award
Photo: Luigi Cuberli

Mountainview College Learning Center
Photo: Clifton Pines

El Centro College is an outstanding example of preservation of historic architecture. This downtown campus was established in a renovated turn-of-the-century department store. Ironically, the Community College District was faced with the need to demolish other outstanding old buildings to expand its downtown campus. The new facilities will join the original one in a remarkably successful urban college.

Eastfield College is seen from a principal freeway across a hundred acres of campus. With their sloping tile roofs and stucco walls, the compactly set buildings resemble a village and effectively project an atmosphere of community.

Mountain View College, on West Illinois, is far from its accessing streets and rims the edges of a deep ravine, bridging across as necessary. Conceived as a "shopping center" for education, it has broad corridors resembling malls, fully connected to form a single white-brick building with subtle interiors and colorful furniture.

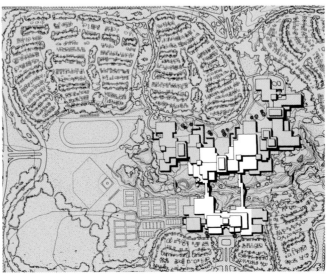

Mountainview College
Master Plan Ultimate Phase.

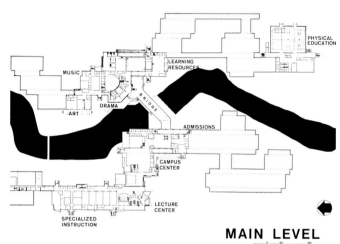

MAIN LEVEL

Richland College Drama Building;
Campus Center Interior, right.
Site Plan, far right.
Photos: John Rogers

Cedar Valley College 1977
Jarvis Putty Jarvis
1977 TSA Award
Photo: John Rogers
Site Plan, facing page.

At Richland College, in North Dallas, a small stream has been developed into a series of lakes that form the centerpiece for two separated units. The structural-mechanical system is expressed in the buildings — boldly, clearly, and ever-presently. Concrete T-shaped frames with dark brick establish the visual motif. Especially delightful is the entrance, which provides a view of the connecting unit spanning the water.

For Cedar Valley College, in far south Dallas County, an intersecting pair of ravines was used to create a 12-acre lake on whose shore sit reinforced masonry buildings. Taking advantage of the terrain sloping down to the water's edge, the buildings have two levels at the entrance, three at the promontory. Ultimately, the campus will occupy three sites, joined by landscaped walks across the dams.

North Lake College, in Irving, is a four-level complex, nestled into the sloping site, with the structures forming terraces down to a small lake.

Brookhaven College is north of LBJ Freeway in Farmers Branch. This campus, the last in the system to be completed, uses inviting courtyards and sloping roofs to provide a sense of shelter. Its hallmark is a windmill, which will generate energy to pump water for decorative fountains.

Northlake College 1978
Envirodynamics; and Daniel,
Mann, Johnson & Mendenhall,
Los Angeles, Design Consultants

Brookhaven College 1978
Pratt, Box, Henderson & Partners
Photo: John Rogers
Site Plan, left.

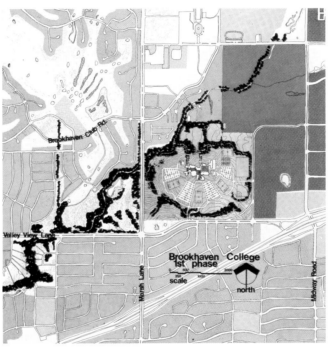

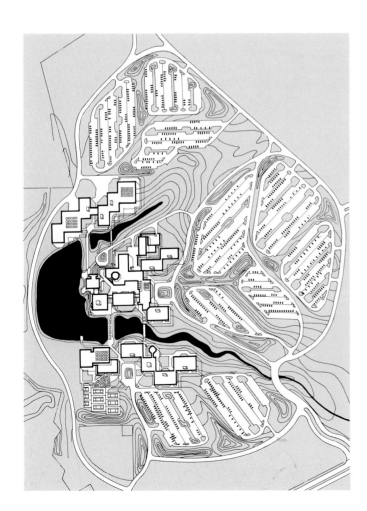

The University of Texas System has expanded greatly in the last two decades in the Dallas area, with excellent architectural results. The campus of the University of Texas Health Science Center, for example, was expanded dramatically when a series of projects was connected onto existing buildings of rather undistinguished appearance and siting. Five firms were engaged for various portions of the expansion, and the new campus exudes the atmosphere that comes only when fine architecture is created.

The University of Texas at Dallas, in Plano, is a new campus that grew out of the Southwest Center for Advanced Studies, an institution consisting of the Founders building and little else. The master plan for UTD was executed by The Oglesby Group, who also designed the imposing McDermott Library and the extension to Founders Hall. Others in this collection of excellent buildings were designed by Harwood K. Smith & Partners; Fisher & Spillman; Beran & Shelmire; and Ford, Powell & Carson.

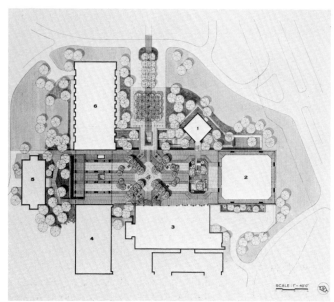

The University of Texas at Dallas
Eugene McDermott Library 1975
The Oglesby Group
1976 AIA Dallas Award
Photo: John Rogers

In the design of buildings for learning, Dallas is moving rapidly from a phase of expansion to accommodate numbers to a phase of improvement to accommodate needs. How effective will this move be? That depends upon the answers to a number of questions:

Will the public appreciate that good schools are more than big, new, imposing buildings?

Will the taxpayers fund public schools adequately, or will they perpetuate the conflict between words, which say, "Nothing's too good for my kid," and deeds, which imply, "Don't spend my tax dollars on fancy school buildings"?

Will educational institutions aim to serve all ages, not just that short span we call school age?

Will educators develop systems of planning that are sensitive to community change — constantly monitoring the relationship between facilities and educational needs, cooperating with other planning entities?

And

Will architects be up to their role?

Will they include in their definition of design their role in the community process, never forgetting, however, that their product is a *building* — a building that fits into a broader scheme, that adapts to change, that makes the work of the educator more effective, and that is an education in itself, doing its share of correcting the cultural and aesthetic illiteracy of succeeding generations?

The University of Texas at Dallas
The Cecil H. Green and Erik Jonsson
Centers 1976
Harwood K. Smith & Partners

73

Chapter 5
Religion

First Baptist Church 1890
Albert Ulbreck
Photo: Doug Tomlinson
This urban church is the largest church in
Texas and the largest Baptist church in the
world, with a membership of just under
20,000.

Houses of Worship

James A. Clutts, AIA

Trinity Methodist Church 1903
James E. Flanders
Photo: Doug Tomlinson
In 1975 this Prairie Style church was
spared the wrecking ball through the
efforts of the North Texas Conference of
the United Methodist Church, AIA Dallas,
and other concerned groups. It is now
listed in the National Register of Historic
Places and the Historic Landmarks of the
City of Dallas.

The development of a religious community in Dallas had its beginnings in the early 1800s when the pioneers came together in each other's homes or in the open to hold worship services. Some local historians believe that the first sermon preached in the Dallas area was delivered by an itinerant Methodist minister named Thomas Brown on March 19, 1844, when he held services in the home of William Cochran of Farmers Branch. The historians will probably agree that most of the denominations were organized and established before 1900 and many were established before the Civil War. The Methodists began in 1844; the Christians (Disciples of Christ) in 1845; the Baptists in 1846; the Presbyterians in 1847; the Episcopalians in 1856; and the Roman Catholics in 1859. Established after the Civil War were the Jewish Community (1872), the Lutheran Church (1874), and the Church of Christ Scientist (1894).

The first church structure built in the Dallas area was a log house 18 feet square known as Webb's Chapel. It was erected in 1846, and later a part of that congregation merged with a church at Cedar Springs to found Cochran Chapel. Although there is disagreement on which was the first church organized in the area, tradition holds that Cochran Chapel is the oldest. In 1868, the First Baptist Church of Dallas, now the largest congregation in the Southern Baptist Convention, was organized by the Reverend W. W. Harris and its original church was erected. The building was not far from the site of the present church.

In 1962, the Dallas Chapter of the American Institute of Architects published a book entitled, *The Prairie's Yield — Forces Shaping Dallas Architecture from 1840 to 1962.* The book points out that Dallas was slow to accept new church forms and that not until 1951, when the Collegiate Chapel of St. Alban was built, was it to have a good example of a modern worship space. Before that time, many fine examples of classic religious architecture were built.

The first building erected by the First Baptist Church at its present site on the corner of Ervay and Patterson was in a modified Romanesque style with Gothic detailing. It was planned by Dallas architect Albert Ulbreck and completed in 1891. The Catholic Shrine of Guadalupe Cathedral (originally the Cathedral of the Sacred Heart of Jesus) at 2215 Ross Avenue is another example of modified Gothic architecture; on this building the brick is handled in a particularly interesting fashion.

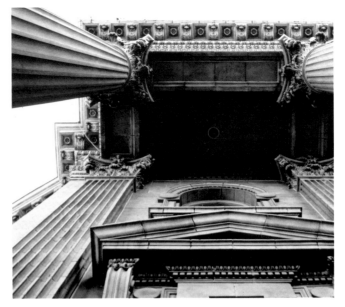

On the corner of Pearl and McKinney streets, pressed hard by paving from every direction, stands what is perhaps architecturally one of the most significant religious buildings in the Dallas area — the Trinity Methodist Church. Completed in 1903, it is a classic example of the then contemporary prairie style, with Sullivanesque ornamentation. Its designer, James E. Flanders, was referred to by *The Dallas Morning News* as "Dallas's first architect." He did indeed move to Dallas in 1876 and remained to make important contributions to both Dallas and Texas architecture. Trinity Church, for a long period in disuse and disrepair, has been converted into a music academy.

The First Presbyterian Church, on Harwood Street at Wood, is a fine example of Renaissance architecture, constructed in 1912, and designed by C. D. Hill & Co.

Two fine examples of Gothic-style architecture are Highland Park United Methodist Church at Hillcrest and Mockingbird, built in 1927, and Highland Park Presbyterian Church on University Boulevard, built in 1941; both were designed by Mark Lemmon.

Other religious structures built before World War II in various classic revival styles include Holy Trinity Catholic Church and the Third Church of Christ Scientist on Oak Lawn Avenue, both Romanesque in feeling; the Episcopal Church of the Incarnation on Central Expressway, the older part of which is Gothic in style; and St. Matthew Episcopal Cathedral on Ross Avenue, which also has Gothic motifs.

There are of course other classic revival religious structures in the Dallas area, but they are possibly less significant than those mentioned.

Trinity Lutheran Church 1960
Koetter & Tharp, Houston
1961 TSA Award

Right:
Temple Emanu-El 1956
Howard R. Meyer, Max M. Sandfield;
William W. Wurster, Consulting Architect,
San Francisco.
1966 AIA Dallas Award
The sanctuary is graced by outstanding art
works of Gyorgy Kepes, Richard
Filipowski, Anni Albers, and Octavio
Medellin.

Lower right:
Oak Cliff Christian Church 1962
Fisher & Jarvis
Photo: N. Bleeker Green

Lake Highlands United Methodist Church
1967
Fisher & Spillman

Except for a few examples of the prairie style, almost all the architecturally interesting religious buildings constructed before World War II were in some form of the classic revival style. This was natural because most architects practicing in that period were trained in the Beaux Arts or Historical Education tradition. After the War, several outstanding European architects, heading various schools of architecture in this country, began to change the training. As a result, there were architects graduating in the late 1940s who were educated in the emerging modern approach to design. With those architects came a variety of building types showing the influences of Gropius, Mies van der Rohe, Saarinen, Breuer, Wright, Neutra, Belluschi, and others. Gradually, conservative congregations began to accept a departure from classic revival architecture. The Collegiate Chapel of St. Alban, part of the Episcopal Student Center of Southern Methodist University, was an early departure (albeit a cautious one, for it is attached to the rear of a conventional, two-story house and can scarcely be seen from the street).

Temple Emanu-El, at the corner of Hillcrest and Northwest Highway, was completed in 1956. It is a fine building, employing simple materials — brick and concrete — in an honest and straightforward way to achieve a design that is an important addition to Dallas architecture. It was designed by Howard R. Meyer and Max M. Sandfield, with William W. Wurster as consulting architect.

About the time that styles in churches were changing, forms of worship were also changing. The altar or communion table, instead of standing at the far end of the worship space, moved away from the wall so the celebrant could face the congregation. The congregation in a sense gathered round the table, and this placed a larger number of worshippers near the focus of the design. Two churches expressing that design approach are St. Luke's Episcopal Church on Royal Lane and the First United Methodist Church of Richardson on West Beltline Road.

The church of St. Michael and All Angels, at Douglas Avenue and Colgate, with one of the largest Episcopal congregations in the nation, is an example of the modern church plant that must accommodate a variety of parish needs every day of the week. It consists of the main church, with a rectangular nave; a new two-story day school; administrative offices; a library; and chapels. Part of it is built around a landscaped courtyard.

Holy Cross Lutheran Church 1962
George Christensen

Upper far left:
First United Methodist Church of Richardson 1965
Clutts & Parker
Photo: N. Bleeker Green

Lovers Lane United Methodist Church 1972
Thomas E. Stanley & Associates

Left:
St. Michael & All Angels Episcopal Church 1963
Harwood K. Smith & Partners
Photo: John Rogers

Holy Spirit Catholic Church 1977
The Pierce-Lacey Partnership
Photo: George Cole

One of the most innovative designs in the Dallas area is that of St. Stephen United Methodist Church in Mesquite. This church was designed by Pratt, Box & Henderson and was completed in 1962. The church is free-form in plan, simply executed. The walls are loadbearing and unusual in construction. They were built of concrete blocks stacked dry, one upon the other to full height. The stacked blocks were then coated inside and out with blown cement plaster and epoxy resin, and reinforced in application with fiber glass. This was the first use of the method in the region.

There are a large number of members in but a few Jewish temples and synagogues in the area. The most recently completed facility houses the Temple Shalom Congregation at the corner of Hillcrest and Alpha Road in North Dallas. Temple Shalom has a membership of five hundred and is housed in a building of modern design but traditional/transitional feeling and concept.

Temple Shalom 1973
Clutts & Parker
Photo: N. Bleeker Green

Right:
St. Stephen United Methodist Church
1962
Pratt, Box, Henderson & Partners
1964 TSA Award
Photo: Bill Boggs

Lake Park Presbyterian Church
(Cumberland) 1973
Gene Hildinger & Associates

Just a few blocks north of Temple Shalom on Hillcrest Road is the Episcopal Church of the Transfiguration. Here is another interesting worship space with a Latin-cross plan, using brick interior and exterior walls, beautifully designed with a modern feeling, but reminiscent of Gothic forms.

Another noteworthy religious building is the Unitarian church, at Normandy and Preston Road. This church, completed in 1964, was designed by Harwell Hamilton Harris, with Beran & Shelmire as associated architects. The planning is significant and the solution highly successful on a tight suburban site.

Modern religious architecture in the Dallas area has just about gone through its adolescent years and is now ready to move into maturity. There may never be another large and noteworthy religious facility built in good classic revival tradition in our area. There are many architects in our community who have, through education and experience, equipped themselves to produce fine religious architecture in the "modern style." These architects are sensitive to the natural environment of our area, to the worship needs of the various congregations, and to the inherent aesthetic appeal of good modern architecture and good religious art in a well executed design.

Architects now have available to them structural techniques that allow innovative design solutions. There will be many forms that will naturally enclose plans for the worship experience. There will be congregations who want an auditorium setting; there will be those who prefer the more formal nave, chancel, transept plan; and there will be those who want to participate directly in the worship service and to involve the choir and the clergy more directly as a part of the congregation itself. These various settings will continue to affect the form of new religious architecture. Also influencing the religious architecture in our area will be day schools, day-care centers, halfway houses, athletic facilities, and similar elements that were not considered a part of the religious community's responsibility a generation or so ago. And, finally, art is again playing an important and proper role in architecture. Outstanding examples of work by such artists as Charles Umlauf, Octavio Medellin, Cecil Casebier, and Bill Jamison are to be found in religious buildings throughout the area.

Dr. W. A. Criswell, pastor of the largest congregation in Dallas, on the occasion of a historical drama, led the benediction. Part of his prayer was this: "O God, may the review of the past be but the introduction to a more glorious future. May we have but begun what God is able to do through us." Dr. Criswell was speaking to the assembled congregation, but his words are highly appropriate for Dallas architects.

Church of the Transfiguration 1970
Beran & Shelmire
Photo: John Rogers

Left:
Thanks-Giving Square Chapel 1977
Johnson/Burgee, New York
Photo: Doug Tomlinson

Unitarian Church 1964
Harwell Hamilton Harris and Beran & Shelmire, Associated Architects

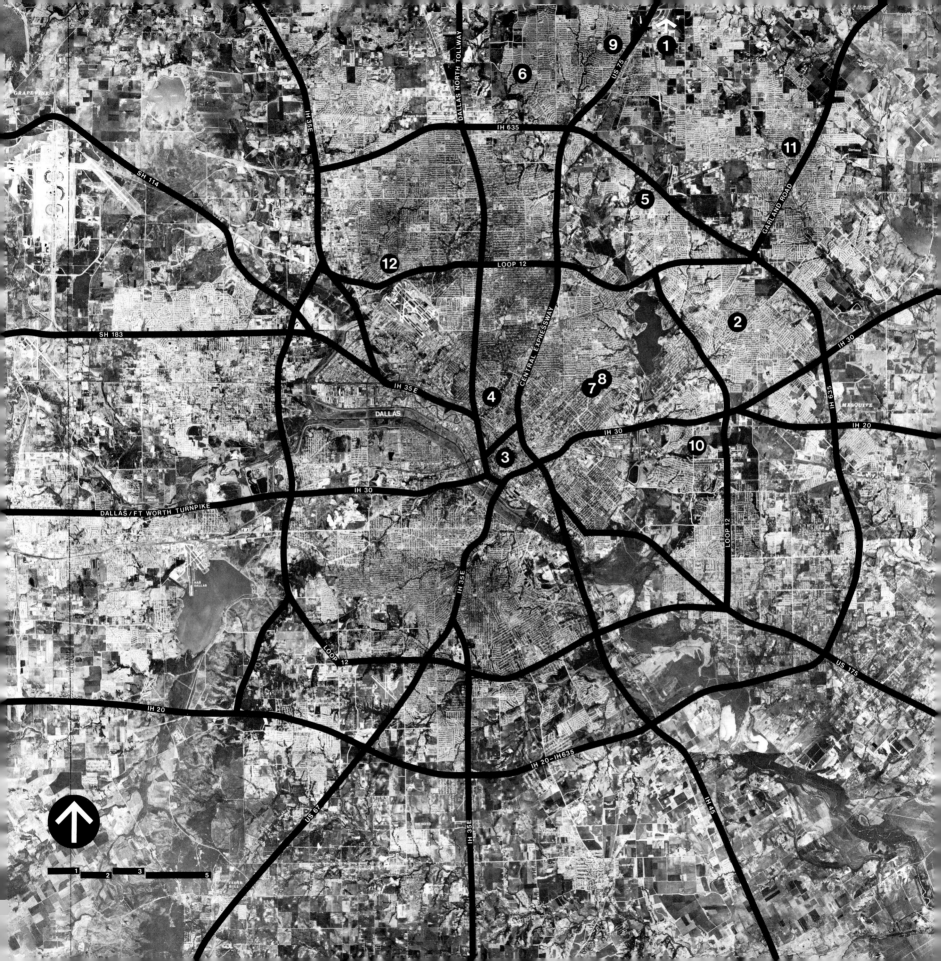

Chapter 6
Government

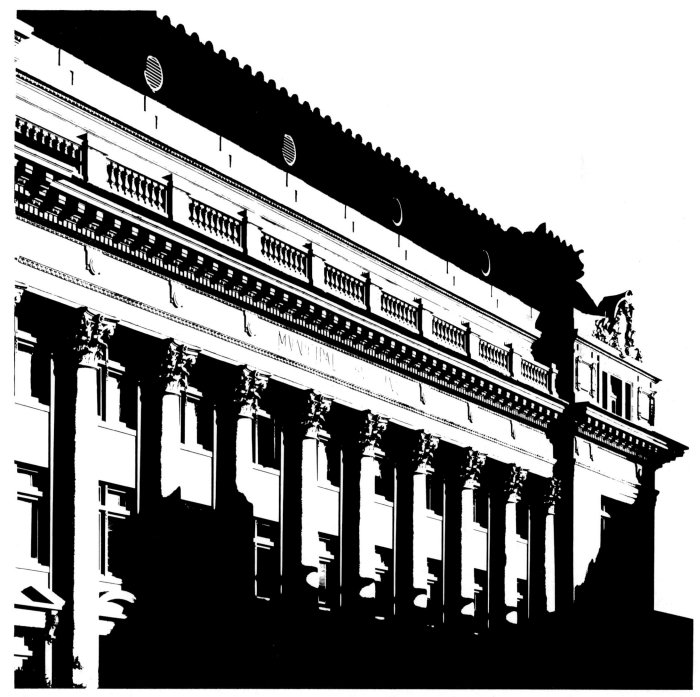

Dallas City and County Buildings

Terrell R. Harper, FAIA

As the population grows and as the demand increases for services from government, the buildings owned, operated and maintained by the public in the Dallas metropolitan area inevitably increase in number, size and complexity. A brief history of those types of buildings bears this out.

The Dallas County Courthouse at Commerce and Hous-ton Streets, a white marble and precast concrete building, is Dallas' eighth seat of County Government. Despite its newness, it must still be supplemented by the County Records Building at Main and Record, the Criminal Courts Building at Main and Houston, and parts of the "Southern German Romanesque" seventh Courthouse at Commerce and Houston. It is also supplemented by eight new sub-courthouses (branches) in the County towns of Farmers Branch, Garland, Grand Prairie, Irving, Lancaster, Mesquite, Oak Cliff, and Richardson, all designed by the same consortium of architects that designed the main Courthouse.

The John Neely Bryan log cabin, now relocated to the County Plaza at Elm and Market Streets but orginally constructed on the block now occupied by "The Old Red Courthouse," served as the second Dallas County Court-house (1848-1850). Both its predecessor and its immediate successor were destroyed by fire. In 1855, a two-story Courthouse fifty feet square, "to be built of the best brick that could be manufactured in the County, and to be covered by the best quality of lead roofing," was designed and built on the Courthouse Square by John J. Good. It was condemned as unsafe in 1871, and torn down. Its successor, constructed of native granite quarried about six miles east of the City, was two stories high, "crowned by a splendid dome," and was built by James Donegan. All of the building except the exterior walls went up in flames in 1880. It was rebuilt, and a third story added, with a mansard roof and a large, square clock tower. The entire structure burned down in 1890, to be eventually replaced by the seventh court-house, Old Red, which still survives. In 1919, the 200-foot tower and two of the four original terra cotta gargoyles were removed from Old Red, and in 1966 the building was remodeled.

The new Dallas Municipal Administration Center at Marilla, Akard, Canton, and Ervay Streets, is the City's seventh City Hall. The first City Hall, constructed by a Mr. Caplin in 1873 at the southwest corner of Main and Akard Streets, was a two-story frame building measuring 60 feet by 30 feet; it had "walk-up wooden steps, kerosene lights and open-hearth fireplaces." A two-story brick build-ing at the northwest corner of Commerce and Lamar Streets, with a fire station on the ground floor, housed the municipal government from 1881 through 1889. The third City Hall (1890; A. B. Bristol and C. A. Gill), containing "all of the conveniences of the day, including running water and gas lights," and also with a fire station on the ground floor, stood at the northwest corner of Commerce and Akard Streets. It was razed in 1910 to make way for the construction of the Adolphus Hotel. Until a new Hall could be built the seat of City Government was a former residence on the north side of Commerce Street, between St. Paul and Harwood.

Dallas County Courthouse 1893
Orlopp & Kusener
Remodeling 1966: Moffatt D. Adams
Photo: Doug Tomlinson
"Old Red" is the only prominent Romanesque Revival building left standing in Dallas. It is listed in the National Register of Historic Places.

Union Terminal 1916
Jarvis Hunt, Chicago.
Photo: Doug Tomlinson
The facade of custom-made white glazed brick is a direct derivative of the Chicago "White City" Columbian Exposition of 1893. Closed to passenger traffic in 1969, it is now an integral part of ReUnion, a large-scale urban development. This building is in the National Register of Historic Places and the list of Historic Landmarks of the City of Dallas.

The fifth Dallas City Hall, a fine Classic Revival structure of Indiana limestone, was built at Harwood and Main Streets in 1914. It now serves as the Police and Municipal Courts Building. After forty years the City Hall had become inadequate, so a limestone and glass annex was constructed adjoining and immediately east of it, extending from Main Street to Commerce. But it was too little and too late from the first day it was occupied. The site for the new Municipal Administration Center was purchased in 1965, and the architects were commissioned in January 1966. Funds for its construction were voted in 1967, but construction did not begin until February 1972. Even the 750,000 square feet of the new building (twelve years in the planning and construction) continues to require supplementation by some 375,000 square feet of other, dispersed quarters for such Municipal Departments as Public Works, Building Services, and Streets & Sanitation, as well as Police and Courts and the essential Water Department technical and shop buildings. The new City Hall was described in some detail, both physically and philosophically, in Ada Louise Huxtable's highly complimentary article in the November 1976 edition of the New York Times. A three-member cast bronze colossal sculpture by Sir Henry Moore has been commissioned for the City Hall Plaza.

Above:
Federal Reserve Bank 1921
Graham, Anderson, Probst and White, Chicago.
Addition 1960: Grayson Gill.
Upper photo: Doug Tomlinson
One of the few remaining Neoclassic buildings in Dallas. Its presence lends a welcome historical texture to the southern side of downtown. It was recently placed on the list of Historic Landmarks of the City of Dallas.

Left:
City Hall 1914
Mauran, Russell & Crowell, St. Louis; and C. D. Hill.
Photo: Doug Tomlinson
Currently the Police & Municipal Courts Building.

Lakewood Branch Library 1969
Fisher & Spillman
1970 AIA Dallas Award
Photo: Richard Payne

Upper right:
Casa View Branch Library 1965
William H. Hidell
1966 TSA Award
1966 AIA/ALA Award

Walnut Hill Branch Library 1961
Fisher & Jarvis
Photo: N. Bleeker Green

Lakewood Branch Library 1937
Lucius O'Bannion
Photo: Courtesy Drury B. Alexander
Originally it shared the building with
Cabell's Ice Cream Store. In the 1970s a
group of East Dallas businessmen
purchased the building to save it from
demolition.

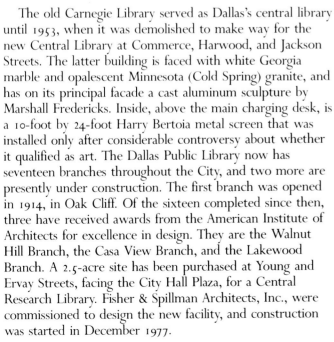

Far left:
Skyline Branch Library 1976
The Architects Partnership

Left:
Fretz Park Branch Library 1975
The Pierce-Lacey Partnership
Photo: George Cole

Richardson Public Library 1970
Jarvis Putty Jarvis
1971 TSA Award
1972 AIA/ALA Award
Photos: Richard Payne

The old Carnegie Library served as Dallas's central library until 1953, when it was demolished to make way for the new Central Library at Commerce, Harwood, and Jackson Streets. The latter building is faced with white Georgia marble and opalescent Minnesota (Cold Spring) granite, and has on its principal facade a cast aluminum sculpture by Marshall Fredericks. Inside, above the main charging desk, is a 10-foot by 24-foot Harry Bertoia metal screen that was installed only after considerable controversy about whether it qualified as art. The Dallas Public Library now has seventeen branches throughout the City, and two more are presently under construction. The first branch was opened in 1914, in Oak Cliff. Of the sixteen completed since then, three have received awards from the American Institute of Architects for excellence in design. They are the Walnut Hill Branch, the Casa View Branch, and the Lakewood Branch. A 2.5-acre site has been purchased at Young and Ervay Streets, facing the City Hall Plaza, for a Central Research Library. Fisher & Spillman Architects, Inc., were commissioned to design the new facility, and construction was started in December 1977.

Left:
U.S. Post Office, Garland, 1977
Pratt, Box, Henderson & Partners
1977 AIA Dallas Award
Photo: John Rogers

Below:
Allen Fire Station 1970
The Oglesby Group; Oglesby, Wiley,
Halford
1971 AIA Dallas Award
1972 TSA Award

The City's first fire station, a frame building on the Courthouse square, was destroyed by fire in September 1887, while the firemen were watching a circus parade. A fire station occupied the ground floor of the second Dallas City Hall and its successor was the lower floor of the third City Hall. The Central Fire Station, at 2111 Main Street, remains the headquarters station for the Dallas Fire Department, but has not actually housed fire-fighting equipment since 1963. Fire Station No. 5, built in 1908 at Commerce and Parry Streets, is now the Dallas Firefighters' Museum, founded in 1972. Included in the exhibits is "Old Tige," an early steam engine purchased by the Department in 1884. Station No. 11, at Cedar Springs Road and Reagan Street, was Station No. 2 at the time it was built in 1909, and a movement is under way to have it declared a Historical Monument. Station No. 5 (the Museum) and Station No. 6, since razed to make way for South Central Expressway, were of similar design, and probably the work of the same architect. The first fifteen stations built were designed for horse-drawn equipment and steam engines, and each contained a hayloft and a coal bin. Although no longer used as a fire station, No. 15 (1917; architect unknown), still stands at North Bishop Avenue and Davis Street in Oak Cliff. Fire Station No. 1, constructed in 1908 at McKinney Avenue and Leonard Street, was torn down many years ago. Between 1951 and 1959, Raymond A. Smith, a Dallas architect, designed several fire stations. Of those, Station No. 34 (the number signifies the chronological sequence, not of the building's design or construction, but of the equipment housed in it), at 8003 Lake June Road (1953) was at that time considered by D. F. D. authorities to be the ultimate in functional planning. Consequently, the architects for the next several stations were instructed to incorporate its floor plan, without significant alteration, in their designs. That limitation was subsequently relaxed, and Dallas Fire Stations designed in recent years have profited by more innovative planning. Station No. 58, recently completed at Irving Boulevard and Harvester Road, utilizes solar energy for heating and cooling. Although Station No. 62 is nearing completion, it will be one of only forty-five operating fire stations in Dallas, and will be renumbered No. 1, as the Department begins to fill the gaps in its present system of numbers.

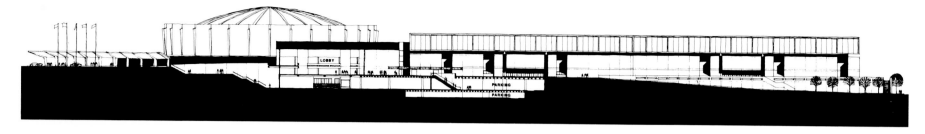

Dallas Convention Center 1973
Omniplan Architects Harrell +Hamilton
1974 AIA Dallas Award
1974 TSA Award
Photo: Dan Hatzenbuehler

Dallas did not have a municipal auditorium until 1956. Memorial Auditorium, at Akard and Canton Streets, comprises a circular 10,000-seat arena, with a 150,000-square-foot exhibit area under it and a 300-seat theater connected to and adjoining it. The Convention Center, comprising 41 meeting rooms and 610,000 square feet of exhibit space, wraps around the north and west sides of the Auditorium. The complex provides adequate space under one roof for the largest of conventions, with contiguous underground parking for 2,000 cars.

Studies are presently being made of the feasibility of a new Performing Arts Center, and of a multipurpose sports and entertainment facility adequate to house professional basketball and hockey teams, as well as other affairs involving large gatherings of spectators. Both of these facilities will undoubtedly materialize within the next few years.

Civic buildings in Dallas County are at long last beginning to be architecturally significant. The trend, with luck, will continue, and Dallas will achieve excellence in the design of its public buildings as it has in so many other facets of its character as a City of Importance.

As a footnote to this chapter, it seems worthwhile to discuss some of the factors that bear upon the design of public buildings, particularly the design of a large City Hall — specifically the new Dallas Municipal Administration Center.

The variety of building types included under the basic identification of Governmental and Public Buildings precludes any in-depth review of the factors that affect how one approaches the design of each. The evolving needs of the user, as well as other design criteria, demand that in designing libraries and museums (the latter category itself embracing a wide range of building purposes) architects be aware of those evolving needs and remain flexible to respond to them. Innovations in building materials and techniques tend to promote a functional or contemporary — rather than a traditional or derivative — approach to the design of auditoriums and other facilities for large gatherings of people. The requirements of fire stations and courthouses tend to change less, except where detention facilities must be incorporated in seats of County government. For smaller communities, even City Halls have fairly static functional needs.

The City Hall of a large city, however, presents a different set of problems and requirements. It is, of necessity, a dynamic structure. Demands upon municipal government change and grow with such rapidity, and political developments exert so important an influence on the use of the facility, that the City Hall architect must be alert to an almost constant flow of revised requirements. Most elected municipal officials serve two-year terms and consequently are almost continuously running for office, with the result that they insist upon facilities capable of responding to the changing demands of their constituencies. The advent of single-member districts for Council members, and the effect of an increasing number of women and minority representatives on the City Council both have an unpredictable impact on building needs, which influences the planning and design of the Municipal Administration Center. The twelve-year span of time from the commissioning of architects to its occupancy is perhaps unique to the new Dallas City Hall. Certainly that length of time has seen many revisions in the internal arrangement of offices, work stations, public spaces, and mechanical and electrical systems. During that period, Dallas has had four Mayors, three City Managers, two increases in the number of Council members (the mind boggles at the total count in those twelve years), several reshufflings of departmental responsibilities, and a doubling in the total number of employed personnel. Revisions in taxing procedures and a multitude of other changes in municipal government functions made it a tight race to finish designing by the time actual construction was completed. And it is probably true that although the building is occupied and functioning, its design is still not final. In fact, the schematic of at least the shell of an expansion building — not to be needed, it is hoped, for another quarter century — has already been designed. Specifically what functions it will house, or how, very likely will not be finally determined until after it, too, is built.

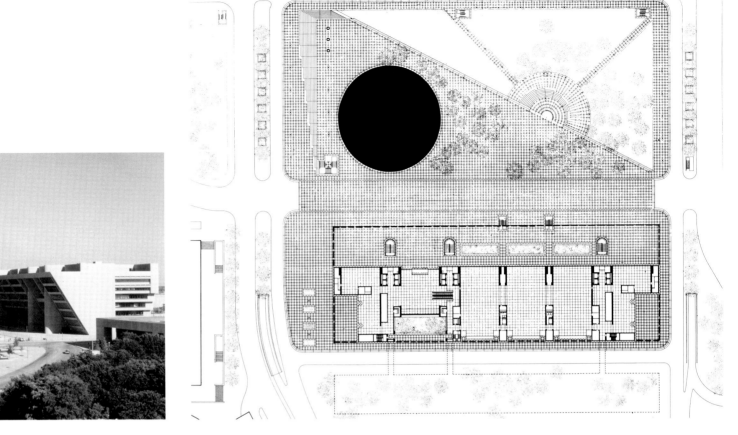

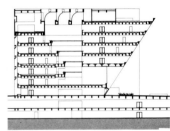

*Dallas Municipal
Administration Center 1978
I.M. Pei & Partners, New York;
Harper & Kemp, Associated Architects.
Photos: Dennis Brack
This cast-in-place building set demanding
standards for the concrete form work,
allowing only 1/16-inch tolerance.
Architecture critic Ada Louise Huxtable,
has said that it promises to be one of the
most important buildings in the country.*

Chapter 7
Parks & Recreation

A Selection of Parks

L. B. Houston

When the steel-rail line pushed northward from Houston and the Gulf Coast in 1872, and another extended westward from the East in 1873, the village of Dallas became a thriving trade center. The population increased, and so did the affluence. As they became better able to afford them, people began to think of the niceties they had previously had to deny themselves. A better residential section grew southward from the original village, and the citizens recognized a need for a public park area. As a result, in 1876 Dallas acquired its first park, City Park.

A combination of conditions brought about City Park, and the method by which it was acquired persists in some form to this day. There was to the south of the town a ten-acre tract on which was a good source of potable water, Browder Springs, that served as a public water supply. The owners offered to sell it, but the City had no funds to buy it, and could offer in trade only an "abandoned pest-house site." Then a public-spirited citizen offered a gift of $200 cash. The gift, in addition to the pest-house site and an agreement by the City to waive for four years in advance the taxes on other property owned by the sellers, was enough to consummate a deal.

That original park, with six acres added a few years later, constitutes what is now Old City Park, across Thornton Freeway from the Convention Center and some five blocks to the east. During the 100 years of its existence, City Park has had a number of uses. It was once the site of a city zoo. Roadways were built through it for buggies and surries; and when a bandstand was added it became the central picnic and outdoor celebration grounds for the City. Then it became a botanical garden and the site of the first city greenhouses. From 1914 until quite recently it was a public recreation center, with facilities for tennis, swimming, and baseball, and a small community building.

Some eight years ago City Park was chosen as the site for an outdoor museum that would encompass a collection of buildings reflecting the early days of Dallas County. A joint venture of the City of Dallas and the Dallas County Heritage Society has made possible the relocation and restoration of a variety of old houses and barns, a church, a school, a hotel, a depot and section-foreman's house, and other typical buildings. Guided tours conducted by volunteers, a lunch-time restaurant serving authentic turn-of-the-century food, and a variety of programmed activities make it an appealing park and a point of unusual interest within walking distance of the Convention Center and Downtown Dallas.

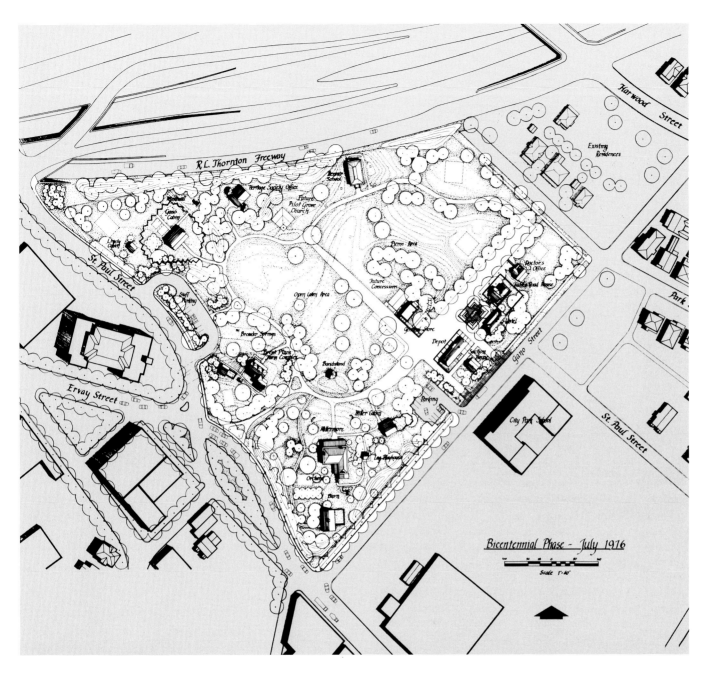

Bicentennial Phase – July 1976

Scale 1'=40'

Old City Park entry gate
Hotel c. 1898

Old City Park
Bicentennial Phase Site Plan 1976
Burson, Hendricks & Walls
1976 TSA Award

Lower far left:
Renner School c. 1888
Restoration 1976:
Burson, Hendricks & Walls

Lower center left:
Fisher Road House c. 1898
Restoration 1976:
Burson, Hendricks & Walls
Hotel c. 1898 & Fate, Texas Depot c.
1886.
Restoration 1973: Ed Hunt

Below:
Miller Log Cabin c. 1847
Relocated to Old City Park 1968
Photo: Doug Tomlinson

95

Right:
Pioneer Park c. 1850
Photo: Dan Barsotti
*Earliest headstone dated 1853. A portion
of the cemetery was bought by the City in
1871. Since 1951 it has been maintained
by the Parks Department.*

Upper far right:
Thanks-Giving Square

Lower far right:
*Dealey Plaza 1936
Gateway to the city
from the west.*

*Sculpture by Jose Luis Sanchez 1968.
This vest-pocket park in downtown has it
all: sculpture, water, benches, and
landscaping.
Photo: Dan Barsotti*

Pioneer Park is adjacent to the northwest side of the Convention Center. It is a tract consisting of an old Masonic Cemetery, an old Odd Fellows Cemetery, and a public city cemetery. The park is a parcel of irregular ground covered with large native oak trees. In walking among the grave markers one can read the names of the pioneers of the city — names that are repeated on the street signs of Downtown Dallas. Pioneer Park, surrounded by the modern world of the Convention Center and the new City Hall, forms a link with the past and lends an air of stability and continuity.

Dealey Plaza forms the gateway to the City from the west. It is by the Triple Underpass, where the three principal streets of the city — Elm, Main and Commerce — converge. When right-of-way for the underpass was acquired in 1935, more land was obtained than was needed; thus when the underpass was completed, the excess acreage was conveyed to the Park Board. The site is of great significance in the history of Dallas: John Neely Bryan's original cabin was built nearby; the first ferry crossing on the Trinity River was slightly to the west; to the north was the first railroad crossing over the river; and not far away was the site of the first Trinity River bridge. Unfortunately, more readily remembered is the assassination of President John F. Kennedy, which occurred near the Triple Underpass.

Plaques recounting these facts are placed about the park, which is extremely attractive with its steep grassy slopes and native plantings. The peristyle and reflecting pool are interesting as an example of Depression Era make-work architecture executed by largely unskilled labor.

One of the most heavily trafficked public park areas is Stone Place, a mall just 200 feet long and 40 feet wide connecting Elm and Main Streets in the heart of Downtown Dallas. It is an intensively landscaped oasis where one can stop to rest, or eat a brown-bag lunch, or simply people-watch. Architects would find the sculpture, the walkway patterns, and the varied construction materials of particular interest.

When Interstate 45 was constructed some five years ago, a good deal of right-of-way land remained open, much of it under elevated roadways. Through an unusual arrangement between the Texas State Highway Department and the City of Dallas those open areas became part of the City's park system. The Highway Department landscaped the parcels, setting out shrubbery and countless crepe myrtle trees, as part of the construction project, and the City of Dallas then became responsible for maintaining them. This arrangement set a precedent that could wisely be emulated throughout the City, especially along approaches to the downtown area.

Perhaps the most unusual park in the downtown area, and certainly the most expensive, is the one-acre triangle bounded by Pacific, Bryan, and Ervay Streets. It is the recently completed Thanks-Giving Square. The landscaping and surface construction have been handled by the Thanks-Giving Square Foundation, a body funded by a broad cross-section of the citizenry. The City of Dallas participated to a limited degree in acquiring the land, and then financed the subsurface development, consisting of a truck loading and unloading area two levels below grade, as well as a link in the Dallas underground pedestrianway.

The intention of the originators of Thanks-Giving Square was to provide a place of peace and quiet, divorced from the bustle of the city. To achieve a sense of isolation, the land slopes downward toward the center; water coursing down channels and over walls creates a blanket of sound that obscures the noise of the traffic. The planting is restrained but effective. At the western end of the park is a bell tower and on the east side is a small chapel with a spiral tower in which services and programs are held from time to time. The chapel was designed by Philip Johnson.

The most widely known of Dallas's parks is Fair Park, about a mile east of the city's center, the site of the annual State Fair of Texas. The Fair began in the last century as an agriculture and livestock show and through the years has expanded to become in addition an industrial exposition. The original Fair grounds, owned by the nonprofit State Fair Association, was conveyed to the City of Dallas in 1904 to be used as a public park. The State Fair Association retained the right to conduct the fair each year, and with the exception of two years during World War II, it has never failed to do so. Today the State Fair, during its annual sixteen-day period, attracts more than three million people. On the Fair grounds, also, is the Cotton Bowl stadium, which attracts its share of people. A group of buildings commissioned in 1936 especially for the Texas Centennial Exposition constitutes the City's cultural buildings — the Art Museum, the Aquarium, the Museum of Natural History, the Health and Science Museum, the Garden Center, and the Hall of State. In addition, there is the Fair Park Music Hall, which each year accommodates the Dallas Symphony Orchestra concerts, the Dallas Civic Opera, the Dallas Summer Musicals, and various travelling attractions.

Currently under way is an expansion program that will eventually bring the total extent of Fair Park to 250 acres.

Slightly east of Fair Park and about two miles from downtown are Samuell Grand Park, with 100 acres, and the adjoining Tenison Memorial Park, with 400 acres. Together they constitute one of the City's most unusual large park areas. The land is traversed by White Rock Creek, one of the principal drainage channels flowing through the City. Samuell Grand Park is one of several parks left to the City by Dr. W. W. Samuell. (Fortunately, he also created a permanent foundation to provide funds for developing and maintaining the parks.) This one contains a large community recreation building to accommodate indoor athletic events,

social gatherings, craft classes, and games of all types. In addition, it houses a tennis shop that serves the adjoining 20-court tennis center. The quality of the tennis center is such that a few years ago it was chosen for the Davis Cup matches, the first time the event had ever been held on public courts. In the park are six lighted ball diamonds, several of which can also be used for soccer and football. But Samuell Grand Park is best known for its azaleas. Here was the first large-scale public planting of those colorful shrubs in the North Texas area. The extensive gardens are planted for continuous blooming throughout the year. Rarely will the visitor fail to find an outstanding display of color. The park boasts a new swimming pool in an unusually beautiful, natural setting. Parking facilities are extensive and convenient.

The adjoining Tenison Park comprises two 18-hole golf courses that share a clubhouse. Extensive natural wooded areas remain untouched to provide a habitat for wildlife and places of observation for nature lovers. On the periphery of the park are picnic grounds accessible to anyone who wants to use them.

Tenison Memorial Park 1923

Thanks-Giving Square 1976
Johnson/Burgee, New York.
Photo: Squire Haskins
This welcome triangle of open space in the heart of downtown was purchased, built, and is operated by a charitable religious foundation. Two levels below the park is a truck terminal operated by the City of Dallas.

White Rock Lake Park
The lake was built c. 1907 although the shore was not used as a park until 1929.

To the east and continuing northward to a point about four miles from downtown is the 2,300-acre White Rock Lake Park. The lake, conceived about 1910 as a public water supply "for all time in the future," was by the late 1920s quite overtaxed. In 1930, when a more abundant water supply was established elsewhere, the ownership of White Rock Lake was transferred to the Park Board for development as a public recreation area. During the mid-1930s and early 1940s, with the help of the Civilian Conservation Corps under the supervision of the National Park Service, the park was extensively developed. At White Rock Lake the public has access to every foot of the shoreline. A road circles the entire lake, in places running very near the water, in other places separated from it by broad stretches of dry land and reed-and-willow marshes. Trails have recently been added for jogging and bicycling, wide enough even for rolling wheelchairs. Boating is restricted to craft with very small motors and to sailboats. The lake is notorious for its erratic gusts of wind, and it is said that if one can sail on White Rock one can sail anywhere.

There are countless beautiful views all around the park, and one of the most stunning vistas in Dallas is to be had in turning west onto Mockingbird Lane from Buckner Boulevard (Loop 12). Below lie the park and the lake, and beyond is the skyline of the city.

To the east another ten miles is Lake Ray Hubbard, a 20,000-acre water reservoir completed by the City Water Utilities Department in 1969. With great foresight, the Dallas City Council, the Park Board, and the Water Utilities Department set out to acquire enough extra acreage to provide a minimum of 200 feet of park land around the entire lake. With negligible exceptions, that was achieved — in many places the width is half a mile or more — and the public has access to almost the entire waterfront. At the time the right-of-way was being acquired, the land for the lake extended into the corporate limits of six municipalities and four counties. The neighboring cities relinquished to Dallas their jurisdiction over the waters within their limits. This gives the City of Dallas the authority to protect the water supply and to patrol the recreation activities. The other municipalities can lease rights to the park land adjacent to them to develop for their own recreational needs. Any development must, however, conform with the Dallas Park Board's master plan. The several cities, mostly through licensed concessionaires, provide for sailing, motorboating, and fishing.

Across the Trinity River, in Oak Cliff, are some of Dallas's most unusual parks. The Dallas Zoo is in Marsalis Park, about a mile and a half from downtown. The setting is unusually rugged, with outcroppings of caliche and a covering of hardy vegetation: scrub oak, red oak, honeysuckle, cedar, hackberry. In the past fifteen years the zoo has been completely redeveloped with more naturalistic settings for many of the hardier animals and climate-controlled buildings for the more exotic and delicate ones. Compared with many zoos, the Dallas Zoo is small. But the highest standards have been adhered to in both development and housekeeping. It is insect free, litter free, odor free — a delight to visit. An index of the quality of a zoo's operations is the birth rate among its rare animals. In this, the Dallas Zoo can claim a worldwide reputation.

Another unusual spot in Oak Cliff is Kidd Springs Park. On this 35-acre tract is a natural spring, a rarity in urban Dallas, that keeps a small lake at a constant level. Standing at the edge of the lake is a handsome glass-walled community recreation building (designed by Forrest Upshaw, Jr.). Two generous Oak Cliff donors have made available a collection of Japanese outdoor art that forms the nucleus of an attractive Japanese garden, a Park Department effort. Deftly worked into this naturalistic setting are various athletic facilities, creating a harmonious melding of passive and active recreation.

Lee Park on the Turtle Creek Parkway. The city built only a portion of the Turtle Creek Parkway recommended by the urban planner George Kessler of Kansas City.

In the 100 years of its existence, the Dallas park system has grown from the 10 acres of City Park to nearly 21,000 acres distributed among 256 sites. The growth has been orderly because it has been based, since 1910 when the Kessler Plan was conceived, on master plans prepared by competent, nationally known planners. All plans are coordinated with the City's Department of Urban Planning and are revised and updated as changing conditions dictate.

The visual impact of a city rests to a great extent upon how well or ill that city deals with its open spaces. Dallas has been fortunate in having, particularly in recent years, a highly competent Park and Recreation Department, backed by Park Boards that are sensitive and responsive to the recreational and aesthetic needs of the people they represent. At the rate things are going, notwithstanding its less than ideal soil and climate, Dallas can entertain hopes of becoming a truly beautiful city.

Throughout the city park system there are some thirty major recreation buildings. It has been the policy of the Park Board to cooperate with other branches of municipal government in providing needed services. A good example is North Hampton Park in far west Dallas. The building there accommodates not only the usual recreation facilities, but also a Health Center, administered by the City Public Health Department, that serves the surrounding region. Presently the building is being fitted with solar heating and cooling equipment as a demonstration project. If the project succeeds, it may well be the forerunner of many similar ones throughout the Dallas park system and elsewhere.

Upper left:
Kidd Springs Park 1947
Recreation Center 1966
Upshaw, Todd & Roberts

Lower left:
Lake Cliff Park 1914

99

Fun and Sun in Dallas — A Review of Recreational Facilities

Dale E. Selzer, AIA

Although Dallas experiences all four seasons, and there may even be snow once or twice during the winter, the weather favors outdoor recreation the year round.

To enhance the recreational options for the public, the City of Dallas in 1914 built a community recreation building in a park at South Lamar and Corinth Streets, a low-income cotton-milling area. The building provided public meeting and recreation rooms for groups of ten to seventy-five people. However, one of its most important functions was providing bath facilities where people could, for 5 cents, rent a towel and get a bar of soap. The bath operation continued through 1939. Eventually, the building yielded to progress, and was sold and torn down.

Today, the Dallas Park Department has charge of twenty-seven community recreation buildings throughout the residential areas of the city. In those that have been built within the last fifteen years is an interesting feature developed by the Park Department, the "glass core." By placing a glass enclosed control center at the core of the building, one person can supervise the gymnasium and all other activity rooms. A good example of this building type is in Fretz Park, at Hillcrest and Belt Line Roads, where it is one of a three-building complex created by joint participation of the Fire Department, Park Department, and Library Board. All three buildings — fire station, recreation building, and branch library — share a common parking area. To provide a continuity of materials and architectural expression and to tie the complex into the surrounding park area a single architectural firm, The Pierce-Lacey Partnership, was commissioned to design all the buildings.

Upper right:
Fretz Park Recreation Center 1971
The Pierce-Lacey Partnership

Center right:
Fretz Park Library & Recreation Center
The Pierce-Lacey Partnership

Lower right:
Reverchon Park Recreation Center 1976
Thompson/Parkey Associates

Below:
Redbird Park Recreation Center 1971
Clutts & Parker

Other recreation centers available to the public are provided by the Young Men's Christian Association, the Young Women's Christian Association, The Boys Clubs of Dallas, and the Salvation Army.

The YMCA has twenty branches and extensions, from Denton and Plano on the north to Waxahachie on the south; from Rockwall on the east to Irving and Grand Prairie on the west. These facilities provide a wide assortment of recreational programs for more than 100,000 boys, girls, men, and women annually. The "Y's" range in size from the twelve-story building on Ervay Street in Downtown Dallas to suburban facilities with an administration building, meeting rooms, and an outdoor swimming pool. Some typical YMCA branches with gymnasiums and indoor swimming pool are the Park Cities YMCA Branch at 6000 Preston Road and the Park South YMCA Branch serving the inner city at 2500 Romine. A smaller award-winning branch facility, the Arlington Family YMCA, designed by Thomas, Booziotis & Associates, is at Pioneer Parkway and S. Davis Drive in Arlington. This is a simple, well designed building utilizing exposed steel roof structure, exposed painted ductwork, and unfinished concrete block walls on the interior. The exterior is enhanced by a subtle supergraphic Y created by using two shades of textured finish coating on the concrete block.

The YWCA also has an active recreational program, with seven branch locations. The most elaborate of the YWCA buildings, designed by The Pierce-Lacey Partnership, is at 4621 Ross Avenue. It has an indoor Olympic-size swimming pool, a gymnasium, a health club, and meeting rooms.

The Boys Clubs of Dallas provides four educational and recreational facilities in the City. A good example, with gymnasium and indoor swimming pool, is in the West Dallas area, at 3004 North Westmoreland Avenue.

The Salvation Army provides two community recreation centers, one in Pleasant Grove and one in Oak Cliff. Each has a gymnasium and activity rooms.

On Spring Valley Road near Marsh Lane in the North Dallas area is a large sports complex, Loos Field, owned by the Dallas Independent School District. Loos Field has two large buildings: a field house seating 7,500 for basketball and indoor sports, and a natatorium with Olympic-size swimming pool. The natatorium, designed by Fisher & Spillman, has movable glass end walls to provide indoor-outdoor activity during warm weather.

Family YMCA of Arlington 1975
Thomas, Booziotis & Associates
1975 AIA Dallas Award
Photo: Wayne Thom

Left & above:
Alfred J. Loos Swimming Center 1966
Fisher & Spillman
Photos: Richard Payne

Far left:
Central YWCA 1976
The Pierce-Lacey Partnership

The Dallas area also has its own version of Disneyland. On the Dallas/Fort Worth Turnpike at the Highway 360 exit, is Six Flags Over Texas. There are 95 different rides and attractions, including cowboy shoot-outs in the street. Six Flags is lushly landscaped, well kept, and fun for all ages.

Indoor recreation is plentiful at Llove, a silvery and glittering recycling of the old Love Field airport terminal near Mockingbird Lane and Cedar Springs Road. For a one-price entry fee, one has access to an ice rink, a roller skating rink, a discotheque, a movie theater, and a restaurant.

Right:
Llove Theater 1975
Lower right:
Llove Ice Rink 1975
Corgan Associates
Photos: Justin Rollins

Below:
Six Flags Over Texas 1961
Randall Duell & Associates, Planners,
Santa Monica, California
Photos courtesy Six Flags Over Texas.

For golfing addicts, Dallas has an ideal climate and fine facilities. Besides the many public golf courses, private country clubs abound in and around Dallas. Two PGA Classics are played here, the Byron Nelson Tournament in April and the Dallas Civitan Open in May. The Byron Nelson Tournament is held at Preston Trail Country Club, a men-only establishment in North Dallas.

The most exclusive and expensive private country clubs are Brook Hollow Golf Club, Dallas Country Club, Preston Trails Country Club, and Bent Tree Country Club. Others are Northwood Club, Las Colinas Country Club in Irving, and Royal Oaks Country Club. There are many more country clubs in and around the city, with the heaviest concentration in the affluent North Dallas area.

Architecturally, the most interesting clubhouses are at Las Colinas, Bent Tree, and Brook Hollow. Las Colinas Country Club, designed by Harwood K. Smith & Partners, is southwestern in style with a red barrel-tile roof and slump block exterior. The interior is warm earth tones with exposed heavy wood structure. From the clubhouse there is a sweeping view across the rolling championship golf course to the skyline of Downtown Dallas. Las Colinas also has an elaborate tennis complex with indoor courts.

The clubhouse at Bent Tree Country Club, in far north Dallas, is a more contemporary, southwestern-style building elevated on a mound of earth created by digging lakes along the golf course in an area that used to be cotton fields. One of the most impressive elements of the 55,000-square-foot building (designed by Craycroft-Lacy & Partners) is the men's grille and locker area, a plush health club with saunas, steam room, exercise room, and four handball courts. Bent Tree, like several other country clubs (Las Colinas, Preston Trails, and Prestonwood) were built by developers to create premium-priced residential lots along the golf course.

Brook Hollow, a venerable old country club with a long waiting list for membership, is on a beautiful wooded site on the banks of the Elm Fork of the Trinity River. Large old oak and elm trees surround the building and line the golf course. Compared with the setting, the architecture is unimpressive. But Brook Hollow is the site of some of Dallas's most spectacular "society" parties. These gatherings call for elaborate theme decorations, one and sometimes two well known bands, and superb food. Some of these parties are rumored to cost in excess of $100,000.

Upper far left:
Northwood Country Club 1960
Corgan Associates

Upper left:
Royal Oaks Country Club 1970
Craycroft-Lacy & Partners
Photo: N. Bleeker Green

Lower far left:
Willow Creek Recreation Center 1969
Ralph Kelman & Associates
1970 TSA Award

Lower left:
Bent Tree Country Club 1974
Craycroft-Lacy & Partners
Photo: Mark Serold

Chandlers Landing Yacht Club 1975
Dale E. Selzer Associates
1977 AIA Dallas Award
Photos: Dale Selzer

Dallas tennis buffs are especially fortunate; weather conditions are favorable for outdoor playing almost the year round. Municipal courts are scattered throughout the city. At Samuell Grand Park in East Dallas, the Park Department has a large public tennis complex where the Davis Cup matches have been held. Dallas is also the headquarters for World Championship Tennis, which holds tournaments at SMU's Moody Coliseum.

Many Dallas residents have their own tennis courts, some enclosed and air conditioned. There are also several private tennis facilities. One of these is T-Bar-M, near Preston Road and LBJ Freeway. T-Bar-M is a private club with outdoor courts, a swimming pool, and a bar and dining room overlooking indoor courts.

For equestrians, there are rodeos, riding clubs, and horse shows. Complete polo facilities as well as hunter and jumper programs are available to members of the Willow Bend Polo & Hunt Club north of Dallas on Farm Road 544.

Visitors flying into Dallas are impressed by the large lakes that surround the City. The prolonged drought of the 1950's prompted the creation of many of these lakes, all of which are man made. Besides guaranteeing Dallas an adequate water supply, they also provide abundant recreational opportunities. Lake Texoma, about 90 miles north of Dallas, is the largest, with about 89,000 surface acres of water. To the south of Dallas is the beautiful 33,750-acre Cedar Creek Lake, with shores lined with pines, oaks, and hickories. To the east is another beautiful tree-lined lake, Lake Tawakoni, comprising 36,700 surface acres. The lakes most people see when approaching Dallas/Fort Worth airports are Lake Lewisville and Grapevine Lake. On the eastern edge of Dallas is a new 22,745-acre water supply, Lake Ray Hubbard; adjoining to the north is a 21,400-acre reservoir.

Around Lake Ray Hubbard, owned by the City of Dallas, certain locations have been designated by the Park Department as acceptable sites for marinas. At one of those sites, on the east side of the lake, is Chandlers Landing, with a 550-boat marina. The boats here, as in many marinas in the Dallas area, are surprisingly large. It is not uncommon to see ocean-size power boats and sailboats. In fact, the marine maintenance building is large enough to house two 50-foot cruisers. The Chandlers Landing Yacht Club, with 18,000 square feet designed to expand to 32,000 square feet, is one of the largest yacht clubs in the country, and could be called a country club with boating and tennis. The award-winning building, designed by Selzer Associates, is all wood with an exposed heavy timber frame on the interior and a wood exterior accented with canvas awnings. The yacht club and marina, like some of the area country clubs and golf courses, serves as the main attraction for a 350-acre residential development.

When football season rolls around, Dallas feeds its enthusiasm with the SMU Mustangs, playing at the Cotton Bowl in Fair Park, and the Dallas Cowboys, playing at Texas Stadium in Irving. There is not much to be said about Texas Stadium except that it is big and is one of the few new stadiums in the country to be designed solely for football. There are no bad seats in the stadium, but the place to be is in one of the 178 private boxes that circle the playing field in a double-decked row between the lower and upper seating. When the stadium was built, these 16-foot-square boxes were sold unfinished for $50,000. The owners then finished the boxes to suit their own tastes, exhibiting an astonishing diversity, from Louis Quinze flamboyance to Texas Longhorn rustic. Each box is heated and air conditioned, is open on the playing-field side, and contains lounge seating for twelve, a bar, and a closed-circuit television system for the reruns.

As football season enters the play-offs and the slopes of Colorado and New Mexico accumulate snow, ski fever hits area residents. Strange as it may seem, Dallas has one of the highest concentrations of skiers per capita of any large city in the country. To prepare for the slopes, Parallel Haus in Addison has three indoor ski slopes and Oshman's on Northwest Highway has a moving-belt slope for instruction and practice.

Short of indulging in those pastimes that call for extreme conditions, such as iceboating, deep-sea fishing, and mountain climbing, Dallasites can get their fun and sun right here almost any way they please.

Texas Stadium 1971
A. Warren Morey Associates
The roof of this structure currently holds the world's record for the longest clear span: 788.5 feet.

Chapter 8
Residences

Plural Dwellings—The Garden Apartment

Jack Craycroft, AIA

Dallas has the standard assortment of alternatives from which to choose in multifamily types of living accommodations. Although in numbers of high-rise dwellings Dallas is no New York or Miami Beach, it does have several examples of that building type. They range from the Art Deco Highlander on Lomo Alto Drive in Highland Park, a building of the mid-1930s now being extensively renovated, to the architecturally significant 3525 Turtle Creek, designed by Howard R. Meyer in the 1950s. The latter is the most important of the apartment towers that line the west side of Turtle Creek Boulevard, south of Highland Park, perhaps the most scenic area of Dallas. Of two- and three-story condominiums and townhouses there are many examples, but they are of fairly recent vintage, and have got off to a slow start, owing largely to being poorly conceived by developers. Perhaps the best examples of this housing are the Yancey-Camp developments, along Travis and Buena Vista south of Fitzhugh, designed by Frank Welch, and those that have been built by individuals in planned developments like Tealwood Square and Christopher Place. The most significant activity, however, has been in garden apartment projects, with twenty to forty low units per acre. The reasons are obvious: Why build tall, expensive buildings that entail parking problems when there is plenty of land to spread out the units and provide space for the all-important automobile by everyone's front door?

Right:
Tanbark Row/Woodridge Condominiums
1974
ANPH
1975 AIA Dallas Award

Far right:
Phase One Townhouses 1970
Frank Welch, Midland, Texas
Photo: Richard Payne

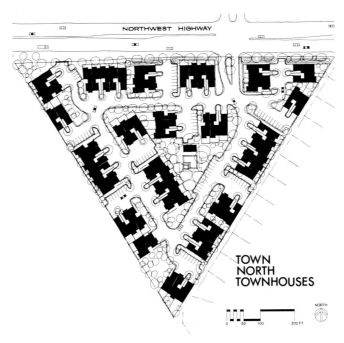

TOWN
NORTH
TOWNHOUSES

NORTHWEST HIGHWAY

NORTH

0   50   100   200 FT

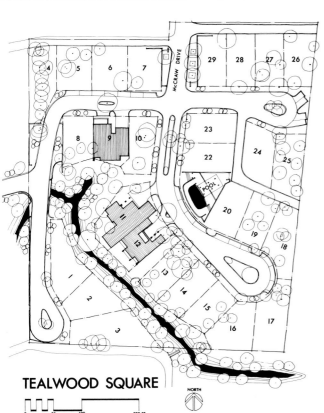

TEALWOOD SQUARE

NORTH

0   50   100   200 FT

Dallas is nationally acclaimed as an important study model for garden apartments. With some 170,000 units constructed in the metropolitan area since the late 1950s when the building type really began to evolve, numbers alone seem to justify this opinion. Beyond that, in a building industry filled with imitators, the architectural innovation in Dallas is significant. A strong market demand created by the population explosion of the 1950s and a changing society that sought alternatives to the traditional single-family house created a new investment opportunity for enlightened developers. The garden apartment was a new building type, and as such it offered a challenge to architects: the way it is designed can influence the quality of life within it and the urban fabric without. To appraise the degree of success of those who responded to the challenge, one must understand why and how today's garden apartment evolved.

Immediately after World War II, apartments were built largely with government-aided financing of one type or another, mostly under the 608 Program. The Federal Housing Administration had its influence on the design, and although the buildings were well constructed, they lacked imagination and livability and generally resembled those on military bases. Densities, by today's standards, were low, and the projects were large. But they did prove there was a demand for multifamily housing in a city that was beginning to show signs of urban sprawl. Many of the projects, such as Preston Village on Northwest Highway west of Hillcrest, still stand, and although new developments have made them obsolete, they still enjoy high occupancy rates because they are well located and the rents are comparatively low. Others have been demolished to make way for new apartments.

From the 608's and buildings in the six- to eight-unit range in older neighborhoods, the garden apartment, as a building type, began to evolve into what today is, at its best, a rather sophisticated piece of real estate. Not only the demand for this kind of living accommodation, but other influences, triggered these advances. A new breed of developer began incubating in the unique Dallas environment. It has been said that Dallas is here "only because its people damn well want it to be." Lacking the usual stimuli to growth, such as transportation, natural resources, and physical beauty, the city was built by a series of entrepreneurs who created an economic and governmental system geared to their needs.

Thus Dallas was ready to respond with zoning and financing when developers like Bill Troth, Lindsey Embry, and Harvey Huie began looking for opportunities beyond the single-family market in which they had started their careers. Others, like Fred and Martin Tycher and Irving Deal, came to Dallas because they recognized the growth potential of the Sun Belt before that was a popular term. Trammel Crow, George Yamini, and Robert Folsom expanded their interests from other real estate endeavors into apartments. There were others; some made it and some didn't.

In the late 1950s, in response to developer requests, the City of Dallas changed the zoning in two significant areas. The first, an area of large decaying houses, was the Gaston-Live Oak corridor in East Dallas. The once-grand homes of Dallas's elite were demolished to make way for the most bizarre array of "Las Vegas Contemporary" apartments imaginable. The new zoning ordinance allowed 36 units to the acre, but the designs were a bad response to this higher allowable density. The buildings were large doughnut-shaped two-story structures with motel-like continuous balconies providing circulation to the units. They afforded little privacy, individuality, or relation to the outdoors, but they had amenities like swimming pools, wall-to-wall carpeting, dishwashers, and central air conditioning. Construction quality was poor. But until better apartments in better locations made them less desirable, they were extremely successful from a business standpoint. Useful lessons were learned on Gaston Avenue, and it could be considered the real birthplace of the Dallas garden apartment.

Apartments of the 1950s:
The Gaston Avenue/Live Oak Street
Corridor in East Dallas

The result of the second experiment with zoning in this period was more successful. This was the so-called Pink Wall Area on Northwest Highway at Preston Road. It was a "planned development" type of zoning that called for larger units at lower densities. The quality of the architecture improved, as did the construction. Because the area was in an ideal location, it attracted older, more stable residents. It has remained a desirable place to live, and in fact, as the apartments have been converted to condominiums, many of them have been bought by the original tenants.

Until the mid-1960s, the city planners and the developers logically theorized that apartments should generally be built close to the inner city. In the early 1960s, nearly all of Oak Lawn, East Dallas, and large parts of older Oak Cliff were blanket zoned for multifamily use. The zoning permitted 36 units to the acre, and required one and a half parking spaces per unit; the buildings were allowed to cover a minimum of 30 percent of the land and were limited in height to two stories. In addition, the standard zoning ordinance called for certain restrictions on building spacing and front, side, and rear building setbacks. The land generally was occupied by houses fifty to sixty years old (old by Dallas standards), arranged on gridiron blocks. Several real estate companies perfected methods of "blocking-up" small lots into larger tracts for resale to developers. Often there would be one or two holdouts on each block, and this established some rather peculiar urban patterns. Typically, there would be two large projects separated by a rather forlorn house. The combination of zoning requirements, land cost, and planning patterns set up numerical formulas that made architectural programming rather simple.

The fact that many of these developments, within the restrictions, afforded an excellent quality of urban life is a tribute to the ingenuity of a small group of young architects who saw an opportunity to build their practices and at the same time reinvolve the profession in housing. The post-war movement to shops that cranked out stock plans for endless tracts of mass-produced single-family houses had discouraged architects from trying to compete, and only clients with the money for very expensive custom-built houses could afford professional design services. Apartments, on the other hand, were becoming far too complex for stock plans; and the projects were large enough that, even at a low per-unit fee, elements were repeated enough to make the jobs worth undertaking. Warren Hall was perhaps the first architect to tackle the problem and he became the first to innovate beyond the early 60's. He designed many of the buildings in the Pink Wall Area. Later, as the boom increased in intensity, two architectural firms, Ralph Kelman Associates and Craycroft-Lacy & Partners were the first to increase the size of their staffs in response to new and larger commissions and for the first time make available to the developers large housing-oriented firms with expanded capabilities in land planning, programming, and design. As other firms also grew in size and capability, the profession in Dallas now stood ready, at last, to influence housing once again.

3525 Congress Apartments 1956
The Oglesby Group
1963 TSA Award

Left:
The Saracen 1966
Ralph Kelman & Associates

Below left:
Walnut West 1967
Craycroft-Lacy & Partners
1968 TSA Award
1970 AIA/HFBL Award

2711 Hood Street 1960
The Oglesby Group
1963 AIA/HFBL Award

The Seasons Apartments 1972
Craycroft-Lacy & Partners
1974 AIA Dallas Award
Photo: N. Bleeker Green

It was at this point that competition encouraged entrepreneurs and architects to develop bolder approaches. First there had to be an understanding of the market and how to respond to it. Because Dallas has long been an airline hub, a large number of airline stewardesses, young male crew members, and other associated personnel have been stationed here. The City's economy is largely management oriented, which attracts many young college graduates. Thus, in the early 1960s, the apartments needed to appeal to the young, both single and married. These people were affluent, mobile, bright, and discerning, and the developments that catered to them were the most successful. They wanted privacy and at the same time an opportunity to socialize. Expensive community facilities like swimming pools, recreation buildings, and more recently, tennis courts, were virtually mandatory. Thus the larger developments — the ones that could support such costs — were more desirable. The units became more elaborate (many had fireplaces, open breakfast bars, imaginative interiors) and strongly related to the out-of-doors with either a private balcony or a patio, and

they had a degree of exterior individuality. The architect's problem was to respond to the demand for those niceties and at the same time to minimize the conflicts created by 36 to 40 units to the acre. Here was an opportunity for imaginative site planning and for thoughtful massing of structures. Some strong architectural solutions resulted. The scale of the buildings became smaller and the exterior treatment in many cases gave something of a village-like appearance, resulting in exterior individuality for each unit. Richer, warmer materials — adobe brick, warm-tone stucco, and natural wood — were used, and the exterior spaces created between buildings became interesting in themselves. No discernible "Dallas School" of exterior style evolved; rather, many strong and varied masses appeared as architects strove for honest architectural expressions of the complex plans necessary to solve successfully the density and privacy problems on the sites. Because of the apartments there, Oak Lawn became a rather unique example of home-grown urban renewal. It was probably too late for much of East Dallas and Oak Cliff to rally because too much deterioration had already set in.

Tolltec Apartments 1968
Ralph Kelman & Associates

Willow Creek, Phase One 1966
Ralph Kelman & Associates
1970 TSA Award

In the late 1960s, the City really began to spread and new centers for employment grew in the LBJ, Stemmons, and Central Expressway corridors to the north. As a result of two more landmark zoning cases, the multifamily emphasis moved out of the central city and followed the growth northward. The first of these involved land at Walnut Hill Lane and Central Expressway. It was a planned development called Willow Creek, the first phase designed by Kelman, encompassing 824 apartment units and an architecturally related retail area. The development includes man-made lakes and a water landscape pattern, structured covered parking, and a private club. Willow Creek reflected the growing sophistication and affluence of the apartment dwellers of the early 1960s who were now maturing but following the trend to later marriages and fewer, if any, children — people who had lived in apartments and wanted to continue living in them.

"The Village" on Southwestern Boulevard, between Greenville and Skillman Avenues, is a group of separate clusters, each appealing to a different segment of the market: young singles, families, young marrieds, and an emerging group, the "empty nesters." The development, built entirely by one company (Trammel Crow's Lincoln Property Co.) consists of more than 3,000 existing units and room for more surrounding a complete country club. The buildings are designed in a variety of styles, and the planning within each cluster varies. The land plan of the entire development, by Sasaki-Walker, was instrumental in obtaining the zoning on the largest close-in tract of land remaining in the city at that time, and it reflected a changed attitude in the community: garden apartments were now an acceptable alternative to the traditional single-family home. There were earlier large apartment subdivisions like University Gardens and Walnut Square, but this was the first for which a temporarily enlightened Plan Commission demanded such a high quality of planning.

Left:
Tres Vidas Apartments 1969
Craycroft-Lacy & Partners
1972 TSA Award
Photo: N. Bleeker Green

Below left:
NorthPark Terrace Apartments 1973
Craycroft-Lacy & Partners
1974 TSA Award
Photo: N. Bleeker Green

The Village, begun in 1969, covers nearly 300 acres in North Dallas. In the center of the photograph is the golf course; at the lower left is a shopping center, Old Town in the Village.

Above and right:
Timbercreek Apartments 1976
The Group

Upper far right:
Old Vickery Square 1975
Manos & Muncey
Photo: Karl Stone
One of Dallas's few mixed-use
apartment/commercial developments. The
apartments and ground-level shops are
arranged around an atrium.

Right:
Woodscape Apartments 1973
The Group

Ja-Lu Apartments 1974
Construction Modules, Inc.;
Myrick-Newman-Dahlberg, planners. This
293-unit project uses 9- by 13- by
30-foot precast concrete modules for all
the apartments. Skillful site planning and
careful designing of the balconies and
stairs give variety to what could have been
a monotonous scheme.

Since the late 1960s most of the activity in apartment development has been northward along the Greenville-Skillman corridor and into the suburban cities. There is also new activity along Dallas North Parkway and in the Bent Tree Country Club area. Although not all of these projects come up to the design standards established earlier, the majority do and in some instances have improved on them. Prospective tenants have some excellent living environments to choose from. Through the years, other architectural firms, such as Wheeler & Stefoniak, The Group, The Architects Partnership, Louis Thomas, Greener & Sumner, Manos & Muncey, Tie Davis, and Murray Smith have made significant design contributions.

If it is possible to make a judgment on the architectural quality of an entire building type in a community, perhaps it should be based on the impact the significant buildings have had on improving the over-all quality of life.

Aesthetics aside, the imitators recognize that, competition being what it is, better buildings make good business sense. Generally they make no attempt at further improvement, and rarely do they understand why the good building was successful; all the same, everyone benefits from their mimicry. In Dallas, all the ingredients — market demand, community attitude, reasonable construction costs, imaginative entrepreneurs and architects, and above all, the competition — were present in sufficient quantity to trigger a twenty-year boom that provided the climate to vastly enhance life for apartment dwellers.

The techniques perfected here have proved to be exportable, and Dallas is known for its significant contribution to the national cross-pollinating of ideas for this building type.

The trend toward fewer children, toward women working outside the home, and toward active leisure time that does not involve lawn mowers is predicted to continue. The response will be garden apartments with somewhat larger and more luxurious units, in some cases designed to be individually purchased. From this trend will arise a demand for more medium-density developments — townhouses, houses with zero lot lines, and perhaps even high-rise condominiums. The developer-produced townhouse will overcome its early design flaws, just as the early garden apartments did, and it will become a significant building type.

The multifamily-building boom in Dallas will continue, for several reasons: the energy shortage will compel people to move closer in and will make it necessary to densify the city; costs of single-family houses will continue to rise. But a stronger reason is that there is now a generation of veteran apartment dwellers. They have become accustomed to the convenience, the care-free aspects, the mobility, the lower cost. More importantly, they are coming to realize that smaller, well designed quarters have about them an air of security and privacy, of urbanity and charm.

The Evolution of the Dallas House

James Wiley, AIA

At a time when most of man's energy was devoted to hacking out an existence on the frontier, his shelter was necessarily of the most simple and primitive construction. On the staked plain of West Texas it was a dugout gouged out of the earth. The upper half of the wall, projecting above the ground, was made of adobe, or sometimes of two rows of small wood poles driven side by side into the ground. The space between was filled with clay or caliche.

The crossing of the Trinity River where John Neely Bryan began his settlement was on the western edge of a band of oaks and other hardwood known as "cross timbers." The wood being more plentiful than stone or other materials suitable for building, it was used as logs for simple shelters for the first settlers of Dallas. An example is Bryan's cabin, built near the river not far from where a replica now stands in the County Park between Elm and Main Streets. Another example is the one-room cabin that was originally used as a school on the Millermore homestead. That cabin, originally built in the late 1840s, now stands in Old City Park.

When a family needed more room, or when two families would live together for protection, two cabins — separated by a breezeway or "dogrun" — would often be built under one roof. The dogrun provided a pleasant place for domestic chores or for social gatherings. A fine example is the Morehead-Gano Cabin (1850) now at Old City Park.

When tools became available for planing lumber, other building techniques began to appear. The picket house was constructed of a single layer of wide boards placed side by side with smaller boards nailed over the joints. Studs were placed only at the corners.

Man cares about his surroundings, and when choices are available he selects the most desirable to assure a pleasant and convenient life. The scenic areas adjacent to the new town of Dallas offered the most pleasant places to live. However, the town, for reasons that are not too clear, was established on the east bank of the river and the closest scenic area was on the west. Because of the difficulty of crossing the river, the houses were built in the areas that were most convenient

John Neely Bryan Cabin, early 1840s
Photo: Doug Tomlinson
The cabin also served as Dallas's first post office and county courthouse.

rather than most scenic, so Bryan's land on the east bank continued to sell.

One exception to the pattern was Millermore, an antebellum house begun in 1855 by William B. Miller on his land grant to the south. The site was on a gentle bluff giving a dramatic view of the river valley and — where one could see through the trees — of the town. The house has been moved to Old City Park and is now restored and furnished with items of its period. It is the best example of Greek Revival in Dallas.

Dallas was growing rapidly in the last half of the nineteenth century. In 1872 the railroads pushed in from the south, then from the east, which allowed the distribution of materials of far greater variety than was possible when the frontier depended upon the wagon train. Fashionable houses began to go up along streets to the south: Ervay, Harwood, St. Louis. Then Swiss Avenue began to develop. Swiss is the best example of a progression of styles in the City today. The earliest houses that remain are in the 2900 block. They are wood frame, generally Victorian, but of a confused and mixed style. Doric columns and other influences of Greek Revival are combined with shingles, turrets, arches, and other forms that were used in a more decorated style.

Millermore 1855
Architect unknown
This house is now in Old City Park.
S. Ervay and R. L. Thornton Freeway.

Houses in the 2900 block of Swiss Avenue. The street (originally Butcherpen Road) got its name when Swiss colonists settled the area in the 1870s.

Right:
Frederick L. Wilson Residence 1896
2900 block Swiss Avenue
Architect unknown
Photo: Doug Tomlinson

Far right:
Modest Victorian houses
in the "Wilson Block"
Photo: Doug Tomlinson

Lower far right:
Residence, 3417 Gillespie Street 1925
Photo: Doug Tomlinson

Below:
Residence, 2707 South Boulevard
c. 1910
Photo: Doug Tomlinson
The South Boulevard-Park Row District
has been named a historic landmark of the
City of Dallas.

As families began amassing wealth, houses reflected more concern for craftsmanship, refinement of style, and variety of materials. In the early 1900s there were examples of Mediterranean, such as the house at 5439 Swiss Avenue and other European styles, as well as examples of the contemporary American Prairie House being developed in the midwest. The R.W. Higginbotham residence at 5002 Swiss (1913, Lang & Witchell) has the horizontal line, detail in trim, and leaded glass, brick, and other materials reminiscent of the Chicago houses of Frank Lloyd Wright.

In 1925 *House and Garden* asked four architects in different parts of the country to design "ideal" houses. The designs were published. The four different styles represented were Georgian, Spanish, English, and French. In Dallas, as in the rest of the U. S. A., the architecture of the individual house continued to be imported. As the City grew, the areas between the arteries that had extended out into the farmland began to fill in with middle-class cottages of a uniform density and style. These early developer houses show an English influence, with steeply pitched roofs, brick arched openings (particularly in the screened porch on the side), and often with fragments of stained glass in the windows facing the street.

Typical of the houses being designed by architects in Dallas in the 1920s were those by the firm of Thompson & Swain; for example, the Orville Thorp Residence at 4908 Lakeside. Another example of the quality achieved in the style is the Anton Korn Residence, designed in 1926 by Mr. Korn, at 3628 Beverly.

Residence, 523 Eads Street 1915
Photo: Doug Tomlinson
This house was constructed entirely of concrete. Note the detail above the first floor windows.

These houses on Merrimac Street are typical of developer-built housing of the late 1920s and the 1930s in Dallas. The open porches are becoming rarer as new owners glass them in for sun rooms.

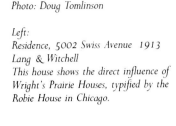

Above:
Residence, 4408 St. Johns 1928
David R. Williams

In the late 1920s, David Richard Williams produced designs that moved away from the popular styles toward the beginnings of a style with regional character. The cultures that were represented in the settlements of Texas — Spanish in the south, German and Polish in the central areas, and French in the east — all contributed building idioms and techniques that appeared in domestic architecture in bits and pieces. Williams seemed more comfortable with the German idioms of Central Texas. Although altered, his earliest surviving work in Dallas is the Warner Clark Residence at 4408 St. Johns, built in 1928. The best and most visible example is the Elbert Williams Residence, built in 1932. The exterior seems to have had no major alterations in its forty-six years. The original interior was finished in brick and in hand-worked wood paneling and trim. A fireplace mural was painted directly onto the brick by Thomas M. Stell and Jerry Bywaters.

The architect who has most consistently continued and developed the philosophy of an indigenous style is O'Neil Ford. Ford worked with Williams from 1926 until 1930, and from that beginning there developed a large body of work. Dallas examples are the Alfred Bromberg Residence at 3201 Wendover (Ford & Swank, 1939), the E. H. Miller Residence at 4717 Park Lane (Ford & Swank, 1939), the Arthur Berger Residence at 3906 Stonebridge (Ford & Lyons, 1955), the Patrick Haggerty Residence, 5455 Northbrook (Ford, 1958), and the Cecil Green Residence at 3908 Lexington (Ford, 1964). The style has continued to depend upon simplicity of form, softness of natural earthy materials, and handmade details for its charm. There seems to have been a gradual shift from the German idioms of Central Texas that influenced the earlier work to the Mexican character of the San Antonio area.

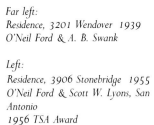

Far left:
Residence, 3201 Wendover 1939
O'Neil Ford & A. B. Swank

Left:
Residence, 3906 Stonebridge 1955
O'Neil Ford & Scott W. Lyons, San Antonio
1956 TSA Award

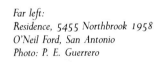

Far left:
Residence, 5455 Northbrook 1958
O'Neil Ford, San Antonio
Photo: P. E. Guerrero

Left:
Residence, 3831 Windsor Parkway 1957
O'Neil Ford, San Antonio
Photo: Doug Tomlinson

Far left:
Residence, 3908 Lexington 1964
O'Neil Ford, San Antonio

Left:
Residence, Coppell, Texas 1966
O'Neil Ford and Duane Landry, Associated Architects
1969 TSA Award

The materials and forms associated with the Mexican- and Spanish-inspired architecture in South Texas were important ingredients in the "ranch house," a style that began to be popular before World War II. The most vigorous and imaginative exponent of the style was Charles Dilbeck, who developed it both in custom-designed residences and in houses built for speculation. A very good example is the R. E. Griffith Residence at 3819 McFarlin, a house built in 1934. Several others can be seen on Bryn Mawr just east of Preston Road.

The Everette DeGolyer, Sr., Residence on Garland Road was designed by Burton Schutt of Los Angeles and built in 1939. It is a more refined example of the Spanish influence in Dallas residential architecture. The owner's sense of humor is revealed in his response, when asked to describe his house: ". . . what a California architect thinks a Mexican peon's house should look like after striking oil in Texas." The house and grounds have been acquired by the city. The house is being restored and furnished and will be used for receptions, meetings, and cultural events, and the extensive grounds overlooking White Rock Lake are to be developed into an arboretum.

Lower far right:
Grounds of the DeGolyer Estate at White Rock Lake

Far right:
Detail, DeGolyer Residence 1939
8525 Garland Road
Burton Schutt, Los Angeles
Photo: Ron Underwood

Right:
Residence, University Park c. 1940
Charles Stevens Dilbeck

Below:
Duplex, 7301-7303 Lakewood Boulevard
1937
Charles Stevens Dilbeck
Photo: Doug Tomlinson
The architect's gift for human scale has made his residences universally popular. His work in masonry detailing is particularly outstanding. Several of Dilbeck's houses diliberately incorporated a sag in the roof ridge beam to achieve a desired softness of form.

Far left:
Entry façade, DeGolyer Residence

Left:
Residence, 4637 Mockingbird Lane 1938
John Astin Perkins
Photo: Doug Tomlinson
This house, designed for colorful Dallas oilman, "Dad" Joiner, is perhaps the best preserved of the city's International Style/Art Deco residences. A number of houses in the Park Cities and Lakewood were built in this style after it was introduced to Dallasites at the Texas Centennial Exposition of 1936.

Residence, 4524 Rawlins 1940
Ralph Bryan
This house, in the notable Perry Heights neighborhood, recalls the comfortable plantation style of the Old South.

Residence, 9400 Rockbrook 1958
Frank Lloyd Wright
Photo: Doug Tomlinson
This is one of Wright's largest houses. The angles in it, in plan, are primarily either 60 or 120 degrees.

121

Above:
Residence, 11207 Shelterwood 1968
Landry & Landry
1970 AIA Dallas Award

Right:
Residence, 3717 Maplewood 1964
Pratt, Box, Henderson & Partners
1966 TSA Award
1968 AIA Dallas Award
Photo: Balthazar Korab

Right:
Residence, 3832 Turtle Creek Drive 1965
Downing A. Thomas
1966 AIA Dallas Award
Turtle Creek Drive, parallel with Turtle
Creek Boulevard and east of Turtle Creek
itself, is a charming street of European
ambience. This house clings to a steep
embankment on the east side of the Drive.

Far right:
Residence, 4606 St. Johns Drive 1965
The Oglesby Group
1965 TSA Award

After World War II, there began a boom in residential building that could not have been anticipated. A home of his own was the dream of every returning war veteran and a grateful nation provided loans to make his dream a reality. The land developer and home builder offered a standard model later to be labeled the "Dallas house": a bland combination of red brick veneer, wood shingles, a picture window, all under a hipped roof, and arranged to look as wide as possible from the street.

With the expansion of the city, residential architecture began to be influenced by the richness of the economy. The designer not only had a palette of materials that had never been available before, he had the ability to completely control the interior environment. With abundant and cheap fuel, Texas led the nation in air-conditioning technology. The air-conditioned house was able to ignore the climatic conditions that had shaped its predecessors for centuries. Since it was no longer important to catch the breeze, the openings were oriented instead to desirable views. The use of glass increased, and in many ways houses became more open. At the same time, privacy began to be more important. The family's social life moved from the "public" front porch to the intimacy of the den or the family room.

The sprawling ranch house continued to be built, even though the reasons for its form were no longer valid. But architects more responsive to the times in which they were designing began to enclose the largest volume of space in the most efficient way, achieving more compactly arranged plans. The Bruno Graf Residence, designed by Edward Durell Stone in 1957, is probably the most impressive example. This house, at 5243 Park Lane, has enough space to elegantly contain both a dining area surrounded by water and a swimming pool. The formal massing is achieved with the aid of a solar screen, foreign to Dallas in 1957, but made popular by Stone.

Throughout its history, Dallas's domestic architecture has been influenced by external forces. Perhaps its location at the confluence of many cultures — the ante-bellum to the east, the desert to the west, the midwestern plains to the north, and the Latin-American to the south — has prevented the development of a clearly identifiable Dallas culture. A hundred and thirty years is not enough time and individual wealth has not been inherited over enough generations for unique traditions to become established, and having no established traditions, Dallas has no established indigenous architectural style.

Architectural firms working in Dallas seemed to be developing personal styles — perhaps influenced as much by published work from other parts of the nation and the world as by the local culture. The Tobian Residence (9612 Rockbrook) designed in 1958 by Howard R. Meyer, and the house designed by Harwell Hamilton Harris at 3504 Lexington are the best examples of the residential work of those firms. These houses exhibit a careful and natural use of materials that reflects the informal life in Dallas (informal by southern and eastern standards). Scott Lyons has refined the same idiom, often emphasizing the horizontal line of the fascia with a strong accent color, as in the Dan Williams house at 3711 Lexington, built in the 1960s.

House and Garden selected as its 1970 Hallmark House the house designed for Stuart Hunt at 5905 Haraby Court. With its highly articulated plan, it exemplifies the work of The Oglesby Group, although the house at 3727 Miramar, designed by them and only recently completed, is in sharp contrast.

Dallas architects are becoming accustomed to dramatic change. Our "spaceship earth" has become so comprehensible by all its inhabitants that cultures have become intermingled. With societal differences becoming less well defined, the force of those differences shapes architecture less and less. The last ten years have seen a startling depletion of natural resources, which promises radical rethinking of architectural form. However, our desire to control our environment and live comfortably and conveniently remains strong; it will continue to influence the architect's approach to design.

Here at the end of the 1970s we have come to a fork in the road: will technology find solutions that will let us continue to artificially control the climate and further encapsule ourselves, or will we look for more natural ways to create enjoyable surroundings? We are beginning to see experiments in both directions; the question of which direction will prevail in the design of the Dallas house — indeed, of houses everywhere — generates the real excitement of living and working in our time.

Above:
Residence, 5411 Surrey Circle 1971
The Oglesby Group, Oglesby, Wiley, Halford
1973 AIA Dallas Award

Left:
Residence, 3918 Normandy 1971
The Oglesby Group
1971 TSA Award

Above:
Residence, 5030 Ravine Drive 1970
The Oglesby Group, Oglesby, Wiley, Halford
1971 AIA Dallas Award
1972 TSA Award

Above and left:
Residence, 3514 Arrowhead 1973
The Oglesby Group
1974 TSA Award
1975 AIA Dallas Award
Remodelled and enlarged twice by the architects, this house is a particularly skillful blending of the original 1930s residence and later additions.

Generally speaking, the visual impact of Dallas is experienced more strongly in large segments than through individual buildings. Here are presented several purely residential neighborhoods that are particularly impressive visually. Some offer rare topography, some are of historical interest, and most present many examples of fine residential architecture. All reflect sound planning principles.

This study is not comprehensive; rather it is exclusive, as are most of the neighborhoods themselves.

Munger Place

The East Dallas neighborhood of Munger Place, including the Swiss Avenue Historic District, contains the finest intact area of Early Twentieth Century architecture to be found in the Southwest, possibly in the entire U. S. The neighborhood is bounded roughly by Fitzhugh, Live Oak, LaVista, Gaston, Beacon, and Reiger Streets and encompasses 140 acres.

In 1905 R. S. Munger, a cotton gin manufacturer, began developing what the *Dallas Morning News* called "the grandest residence section in the entire Southland." Munger had no favorable topography to work with here. The land was flat and bald and planted in cotton, corn, and sorghum. Zoning was nonexistent at that time, so the pioneer developer used deed restrictions to accomplish his purpose. Utilities were placed in alleys, houses were required to be two stories high with a $10,000 minimum construction cost, and only very restricted commercial areas were allowed. The sixty-foot setbacks required by Munger on some streets produced a rhythm of spaces between structures that remains one of the area's most striking spatial elements.

From earliest planning, Swiss Avenue has represented the best of Munger Place. The boulevard has a grandness of scale and an architectural richness and variety that are rarely seen. Swiss was initially composed of two separate streets — one public and one private — separated by a park forty feet wide. Two hundred houses were built between 1905 and 1930 representing sixteen distinct architectural styles. Most notable are examples of Classic Revival, Prairie Style,

Georgian Revival, English Tudor, Shingle Style, and Italian Renaissance.

In the early 1970s the Dallas Historic Preservation League and the National Trust for Historic Preservation combined efforts to fight successfully a proposal for rezoning Swiss Avenue for apartment towers. This team, with support from the Dallas Department of Urban Planning, achieved Historic District status for Swiss Avenue in 1973. The street is listed on the National Register of Historic Places.

"Urban pioneers," attracted by the neighborhood's economic heterogeneity and low per-square-foot house costs, are restoring Munger Place in a manner worthy of emulation. There is a wonderful sense of discovery, vision, and boundless energy to be had in driving other streets in the old neighborhood. On Victor, Tremont, Worth, and Reiger, Prairie Style houses abound in various states of repair and disrepair. Forgotten residences — just months ago used only as cheap rooming houses or apartments — have been bought by enthusiastic young people who are, with meticulous care, restoring them to their original architectural design.

As a result of the active involvement of these determined young residents in neighborhood preservation, lending institutions have made home improvement loans and mortgage financing readily available. The two-million-dollar loan guaranty program of FNMA through Lakewood Bank and Trust is the first of its kind in the country.

The houses of Swiss Avenue illustrate the diversity of style, ornament, and scale typical of early twentieth century architectural taste. As these photographs suggest, very few of them are of a single, consistent style. The variety reflects an attitude of individuality that, on the whole, is lacking today.

The Old Pecan Tree c. 1865
Armstrong Parkway near Preston Road
The developers of Highland Park in 1923
so valued the old pecan tree that they
asked landscape architect George Kessler
to "put the tree in a prominent location"
in his plan for Highland Park West. With
few exceptions, every year since 1927 has
seen two thousand lights transform it into
"the million dollar" Christmas tree, a
landmark dear to nearly every child in
Dallas.

Old Highland Park

Highland Park Village 1931
Fooshee & Cheek
Photo: Doug Tomlinson
The architects visited Spain with the
developers to decide on a style for the
center.

Drive north on St. Johns or Lakeside Drive — either could be the most beautiful street in Dallas — from Wycliff to Beverly. Here in Old Highland Park there is a lesson to be learned about planning. Only slightly unusual topographic features were used to strongest advantage to create what syndicated columnist O. O. McIntyre called "the most beautiful suburb in America."

Turtle Creek, flowing through a series of small lakes in Lakeside Park and Dallas Country Club, forms an open-space spine for the town. Hackberry Creek, a picturesque tributary, has rugged limestone banks and winds sinuously between St. Johns and Drexel Drives among houses and under Town Hall. Tennis courts and the town swimming pool are carved from the banks of the creek. There are stone foot bridges, gravel walks, and picnic areas. These parks are strongly linear, a distribution of open space that touches everyone in the neighborhood. Skillful variation of lot sizes, elegantly curving streets, and well located vest-pocket parks were used to create changing vistas and to give a sense of identity to each block.

In 1907 Highland Park was planned to be special. Fourteen hundred acres of farmland (originally belonging to the pioneer M. C. Cole family) had been purchased by developer John S. Armstrong. The tract was several miles north of Dallas, and Armstrong envisioned a development comparable to today's "new towns." The Armstrong sons-in-law, Edgar Flippen and Hugh Prather, Sr., headed the project, and they hired Wilbur David Cooke, the planner of Beverly Hills, California, to plan the first section — east of Preston Road and south of Mockingbird Lane — now known as "Old" Highland Park.

The result of that planning effort is that today scarcely a house in Old Highland Park is available for under $100,000, and transactions of $500,000 are not uncommon. Building sites alone are so desirable that people are willing to pay up to $150,000 for a house of little value so they can clear the lot for new construction.

In the mid-1920s, Highland Park expanded west of Preston Road. Despite the uninspiring topography, the visionary system of routing streets was retained. Armstrong Boulevard is rivaled only by Swiss Avenue for sheer scale of manicured residential boulevard and homes suggesting great wealth. To visit here in early April when the azaleas are in bloom is breathtaking.

Continuous preservation and restoration have kept attention away from the neighborhood as a historic showplace; yet the homogeneity of blocks of dwellings dating from 1908 to 1930 makes the area as significant a collection of Early Twentieth Century architecture as Swiss Avenue. The town also contains a number of outstanding contemporary houses.

Above:
Houses on Armstrong Parkway

Left:
Turtle Creek

Far left:
Highland Park Town Hall 1924, 1959,
1975
Renovation 1975: Harold E. Prinz
Here, studied Spanish Renaissance details
are on a form suggestive of Eighteenth
Century Texas missions.

Above:
Residence, 4808 Drexel Drive 1956
The Oglesby Group
1963 TSA Award
This small, simple house, is sited on a large
lot on Hackberry Creek.

Williams Park

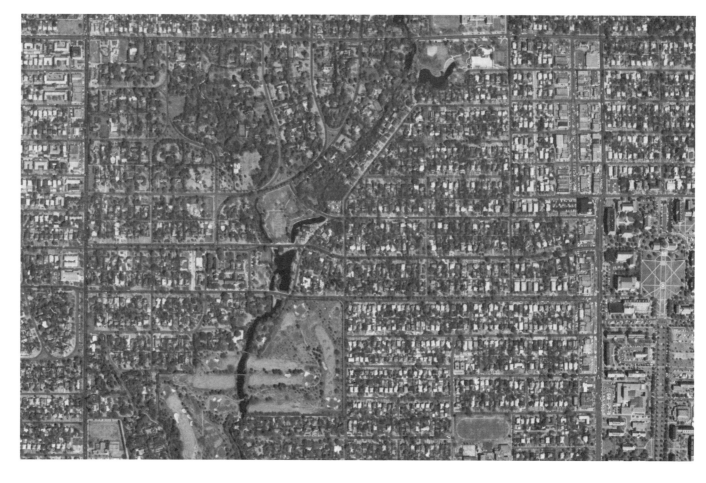

University Park

For many years the city limit signs read, "University Park — Home of SMU, Many Churches, and Excellent Schools." It sounded like the American Dream. And in truth there is probably no more idylically American setting to be found in Dallas than Williams Park flanking University Boulevard. In pleasant contrast, Highland Park Presbyterian Church, with its gothic-detailed gables and rose window, provides visual closure for Turtle Creek Boulevard as it approaches from the north, reminiscent of the studied positioning of the cathedral in the towns of medieval Europe. The church, the park, and the "Independence Hall" style of the municipal building combine to make a statement about life in University Park.

Not all of this island city's 3.7 square miles carries strong visual impact. Worthy of attention is the area surrounding the City Hall, bounded by Preston Road on the west, Southern Methodist University on the east, Lovers Lane on the north, and McFarlin Boulevard or Dallas Country Club on the south. The town began here in 1915 as a scattering of residences near the newly founded university. By 1924 there were 380 homes, many belonging to faculty and all using the campus utility system. The City of University Park incorporated that year after requests for annexation — first to Highland Park, then to Dallas — were denied. Today McFarlin Boulevard from Hillcrest to Golf Drive looks for all the world like a street in a middle-sized Eastern college

town. The crudely landscaped median and the picturesque mixture of 1920s houses — one, two, and three stories high — speak of a continuous student presence and influence.

This portion of the town, like Highland Park, uses Turtle Creek as an open-space corridor. The importance of the creek is most visible in Williams, Goar, and Curtis Parks where it has been impounded and beautifully landscaped. Over a million dollars was set aside in a mid-1970s bond program to renovate the parks and lakes and to develop creative play areas.

Outside of park lands the creek flows unobstructed for the benefit of a lucky few whose houses on Golf Drive and Turtle Creek Boulevard share the creek in their back yards. The scale of house and street increases on Vassar, Baltimore, and Hunter's Glen north of University Boulevard, in the area known as Volk Estates. On lots as large as five acres there are homes styled after country houses of the English Renaissance.

The eight large churches of University Park are landmarks. Highland Park United Methodist Church and Highland Park Presbyterian Church are both reported to be the largest congregations in the world of their respective denominations. In a similar spirit of bigness, the clock on the steeple of Park Cities Baptist Church measures a healthy eight feet in diameter.

Left and above:
University Boulevard

Left:
Residence in Volk Estates

Far left:
City Hall, University Park 1925
Harre M. Bernet

Above:
Duplex, University Boulevard at Preston Road c. 1940
Photo: Doug Tomlinson
Much of Dilbeck's work is in University Park. In the 4000 Block of Bryn Mawr is a small "Dilbeck subdivision."

Left:
View on McFarlin Boulevard

Lakewood

House on Tokalon Drive
Photo: Doug Tomlinson

Rarely does one encounter a neighborhood whose beauty can be attributed to the developer's control over the character and variety of the houses themselves. Lakewood, specifically the historic subdivisions of Country Club Estates, Westlake Park, and Gastonwood, is such a neighborhood.

In the early 1920s W. F. Pearson, owner of rolling land extending north of Lakewood Country Club to what is now Westlake Drive, invited Albert Dines and Lee R. Kraft (with financier S. A. Temple) to develop his property "in the right manner." Dines and Kraft, with a concern for saving trees, implemented a plan calling for deep lots, generous setbacks, and winding streets. Their 1928 development of Westlake Park (the extension of Lakewood from Brendenwood Drive to Lawther Drive) continued in the same tradition. The 6800 block of Tokalon Drive, skillfully placed over a small creek, was called by *D Magazine* the "best" street in Dallas. Lots for a variety of interesting houses climb above the roadway, and large trees provide a dramatic canopy overhead.

The neighborhood's universal appeal can often be attributed to the wonderful collection of split-level and two-story houses, particularly those of a Mediterranean style, along Lakewood Boulevard, Lakeshore, Tokalon,

Gaston, and Country Club Circle. These houses, delightful in both form and detail, derive their character from expressive materials — slate, clay tile, masonry, stained glass, intricately molded plaster, and carved wood. Dines and Kraft, recognizing the importance of architectural variety, hired a number of architects to design their houses, ranging as far as Battle Creek, Michigan, for one young architect with "fresh ideas."

Lakewood's other visual gift is its relationship to White Rock Lake. The proximity to the lake generates significant views and a hilly topography. Lawther Drive, on the east edge of the neighborhood, follows a circuitous thirteen-mile course around the lake. On the west bank of the lake grand estates spill down to the road from grassy hills above. An enlarged replica of Mount Vernon is the home of the late multibillionaire oilman, H. L. Hunt.

The Cloisters, off Lawther Drive near Mockingbird Lane, is one of the newest of the Lakewood area subdivisions, and it is notable because the land planning has helped retain an elegant country setting. The atmosphere is particularly fitting because the land was once part of a prosperous pioneer community of farms that bordered White Rock Creek before the lake was constructed in 1912.

Above:

6941 Gaston Avenue c. 1930
*This turreted house with the unlikely
name Chateau des Grotteaux was the
home of the late Robert L. "Uncle Bob"
Thornton, a former mayor of Dallas.*

*Houses built by C. D. Hutsell on
Lakewood Boulevard in the 1930s. The
living rooms have high coved ceilings with
intricately detailed plaster. Note the
parabolic stained glass window in the
house at the far left. The Hutsell houses
are not so rough-hewn as those of Dilbeck.
Photo: Doug Tomlinson*

6800 Block, Tokalon Drive

6901 Gaston Avenue 1936
*A "House of the Future" at the Texas
Centennial Exposition, part of this
structure was moved to its present site in
1938. Subsequent alterations have diluted
its purity.*

The bluff and the view

Preston Hollow, Bluffview

In 1840, before there was a Dallas, there was a Preston Road — a cattle trail that connected with the Old Chisholm Trail and led to Fort Preston on the Red River. Fort Preston was inundated by the waters of Lake Texoma in the early 1940s, but the road remains, following its historic course north through what are now the most exclusive residential areas in Dallas.

Preston Hollow lies in a low area at the headwaters of Bachman Creek near the intersection of Preston Road and Northwest Highway. It could be defined for the purpose of this study as that area bounded by Preston Road, Walnut Hill Lane, Rockbrook Drive, and Northwest Highway. To the southwest lies the Bluffview neighborhood, consisting of the blocks one-half mile south of Northwest Highway between Midway and Inwood Roads.

In 1922 Ira P. DeLoache flew in a private aircraft over the land along North Preston Road. Impressed with the view and certain that Dallas would grow northward, he built the first home in Preston Hollow, beginning his role as pioneer developer of the area. Today both neighborhoods boast minimum one-acre lots and some of Dallas's most magnificent stands of old trees, rare gifts on the prairie where oaks and pecans sixty inches in diameter are exceptional. The environment for the huge trees was fostered by Bachman Creek and its tributaries. Virtually none of these waterways are free flowing now as the residents have built a series of weirs, dams, and low-water crossings, creating chains of private lakes and pools. One of the most beautiful can be seen south of DeLoache Street along

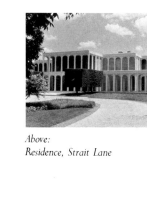

Above:
Residence, Strait Lane

Left:
Shadywood Lane, Bluffview

Far left:
Low-water bridge on Jourdan Way, Preston Hollow

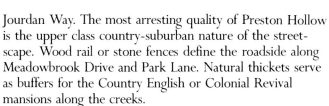

Left:
Canyon Drive, Bluffview
Such soft street edges are no longer allowed by Dallas subdivision regulations.

Far left:
Residence, 5243 Park Lane 1957
Edward Durrell Stone, New York

Jourdan Way. The most arresting quality of Preston Hollow is the upper class country-suburban nature of the street-scape. Wood rail or stone fences define the roadside along Meadowbrook Drive and Park Lane. Natural thickets serve as buffers for the Country English or Colonial Revival mansions along the creeks.

In a city where such subdivision names are as a rule misleading, "Bluffview" speaks the truth. The bluff, visible south of Northwest Highway near Guernsey Lane, was carved at the bend in Bachman Creek. And the bluff offers a panoramic view from the cul de sac at the end of Bluff-view Boulevard. Watauga Road and Shadywood Lane plummet downhill through what once were draws. Trees canopy the streets, and houses cling to the steep banks on each side.

In both neighborhoods the street planning is highly irregular. The bumpy, gravel-shouldered roads angle and loop in unpredictable fashion, sometimes circling upon themselves. The developers created large grassy islands (at Bluffview Boulevard and Cherokee Trail, for instance) where streets curve or wye into each other. Rarely do they simply meet at a right angle.

A glance at income or property value maps suggests that the area exceeds all others in the country in any conceivable measure of wealth. One Preston Hollow census tract in 1970 reported a median family income in excess of $60,000. The architecture is hard to see because of the trees and large lots, but even an occasional glimpse speaks of the affluence of the residents.

Residence, 4668 Meadowood 1973
Landry & Landry
1975 AIA Dallas Award

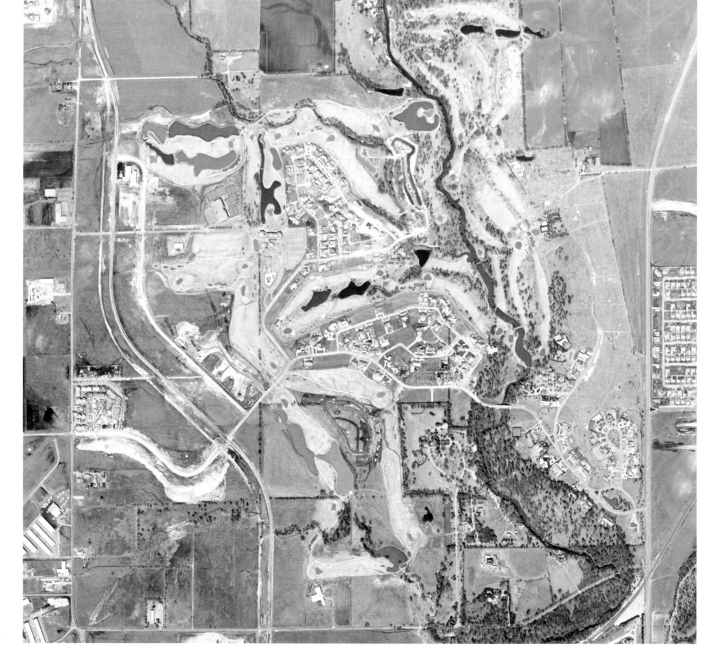

Preston Trails, Bent Tree

In far north Dallas, where urbanization gives over entirely to Collin County's blackland farms, the prairie is still visible side by side with two of the most exclusive country club communities in Texas. Typical of North Texas, the land is rolling and generally bare. Here native trees grow only along White Rock Creek and its tributaries.

The Clint Murchison, Sr., family first bought land on Keller Springs Road west of Preston Road in 1929. The family holdings were expanded in the early 1960s until John Murchison with Stuart Hunt, Pollard Simons, and Jimmy Chambers founded Preston Trail Golf Club. Having admired "The Cloisters" on White Rock Lake, the group in 1965 hired that project's planners (Phillips, Proctor, and

Bowers) to create a prestigious residential subdivision adjacent to the golf course. The planners were charged to develop as rural an ambience as was possible within the constraints of Dallas codes and ordinances, and, since the developers intended to make Preston Trails their home, to control the quality of that semirural environment. A profit on the venture would be only a welcome by-product.

Earth berms screen views into Preston Trails from Preston Road, allowing a dramatic entry into the area at Westgrove Drive. There the visitor is greeted with a view of landscaped parks and small lakes. The parks, tennis courts, and flood plains are managed by a home-owners' association. An architectural control committee reviews all plans

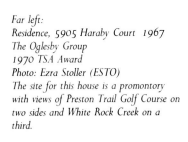

Far left:
Residence, 5905 Haraby Court 1967
The Oglesby Group
1970 TSA Award
Photo: Ezra Stoller (ESTO)
The site for this house is a promontory with views of Preston Trail Golf Course on two sides and White Rock Creek on a third.

Left:
Residence, Bent Tree 1974
Frank Welch, Midland, Texas

Far left:
Residence, Preston Trails 1969
Dale E. Selzer Associates

Left:
Residence, Preston Trails 1970
This house reportedly was built entirely of materials imported from Mexico, by laborers also imported from Mexico.

Far left:
Residence, Preston Trails 1973
Ralph Kelman & Associates

Private park and lakes
Westgrove Drive, Preston Trails

for new houses, monitoring deed restrictions and enforcing guidelines on material selection, colors, size of house, and position on the large, one- to two-acre lots.

Adjacent to Preston Trails and encompassing more than four hundred acres to the west is the country club and residential community of Bent Tree. Begun in the early 1970s by Folsom Investments, Inc., this project benefits from imaginative planning that loops the golf course around pockets of homesites. One group of townhouse sites is on a topographical saddle between White Rock Creek and Hall's Branch. The sites overlook the golf courses of both Preston Trails and Bent Tree and are spectacular. The environmental cues of Preston Trails were taken by Bent Tree: on the

approach road to the clubhouse are "bent" live oak trees, meticulously selected for character and trucked to Dallas from Central Texas.

The houses of the area, particularly those in Preston Trails, are vividly expressive, telling much about the tastes and priorities of the owners. There are many designed by architects; several of them might be labeled experimental contemporary, and a number are beautifully regional. Houses in Preston Trails valued at less than half a million dollars tend to be the exception. This fact is especially significant in a city that generally boasts some of the lowest housing costs in the country.

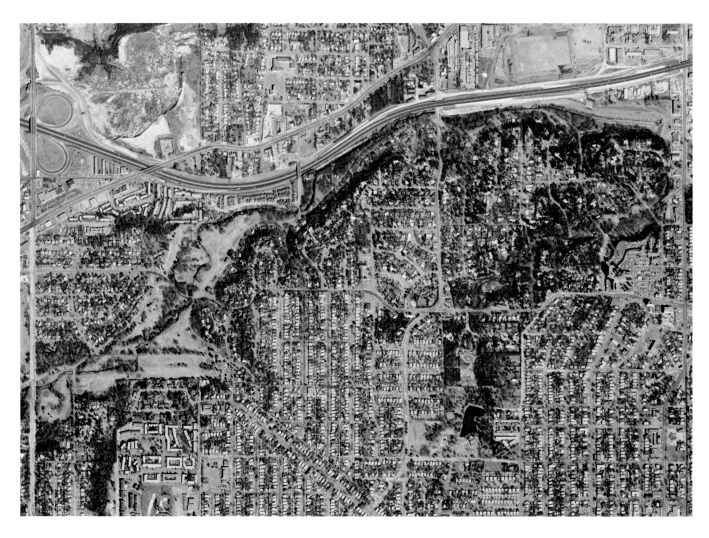

Kessler Park, Stevens Park

In 1908 a devastating flood severed Dallas from recently annexed Oak Cliff across the Trinity River. This led the Dallas City Plan and Improvement League to hire George E. Kessler, a well known landscape architect from Kansas City, to replan Dallas. In his plan were "sweeping portrayals of boulevards, greenbelts, and parks," and a levee system and Town Lake for the Trinity, visions that are still being implemented. Kessler later became involved in planning a beautiful Oak Cliff neighborhood that bears his name, Kessler Park.

The original sections of Kessler Park straddle Edgefield Drive north of Colorado Boulevard and were developed in 1924 by a father and son team, George Owens, Senior and Junior. Kessler carefully looped two streets around the edge of wooded hilltops. These, originally called Canterbury Court and Marsalis Court (now Windomere Avenue and Lausanne Drive), contain the most homogeneous groups of large and well detailed houses of the pre-Depression period in Kessler Park.

Coombs Creek and Kidd Springs Branch, winding their way to the Trinity River, carved canyons through this up-lifted edge of the Austin Chalk. The edges have softened with development and now form the spectacular homesites

of "East Kessler." Roy Eastus began developing the section east of Sylvan Drive in the mid-1930s, haphazardly yet picturesquely cutting narrow streets through the trees. In one block of Cedar Hill Road just south of Kessler Parkway the street is literally carved out of limestone, which towers fifteen to twenty feet above the roadway.

Others carried on George Kessler's tradition in this part of the City. The L. A. Stemmons family land around what is now Methodist Hospital on Colorado Boulevard became the attractive Evergreen Hill subdivision. And in the 1930s Stevens Park Estates was developed as an extremely well planned neighborhood immediately west of Old Kessler Park. Residents on Plymouth Road in Stevens Park have perhaps the best views in Dallas. Their two-story houses, sited on a ridge, have a prospect of Coombs Creek as it meanders through Stevens Park Municipal Golf Course.

Although one doesn't sense it, Kessler Park and Stevens Park are inner-city neighborhoods, lying — by Dallas standards — in the shadow of downtown. Because of this the area is attracting a stream of interested home buyers, particularly those immigrating from the east. The hills and trees of Kessler Park "look like home."

Far left:
Stevens Park Golf Course

Left:
Plymouth Road, Stevens Park

Left:
Residence, Lausanne Drive at Colorado
Boulevard c. 1930
Kessler Park

Far left:
"The Old Rock Lodge"
1622 Cedar Hill Road c. 1900
The original stone structure, formerly a
hotel or "community center," predates the
development of Kessler Park.

Above:
Residence, 1630 Nob Hill Road 1962
J. Herschel Fisher

Far left:
Residence, Canterbury Court c. 1930
Kessler Park

137

Chapter 9
Health

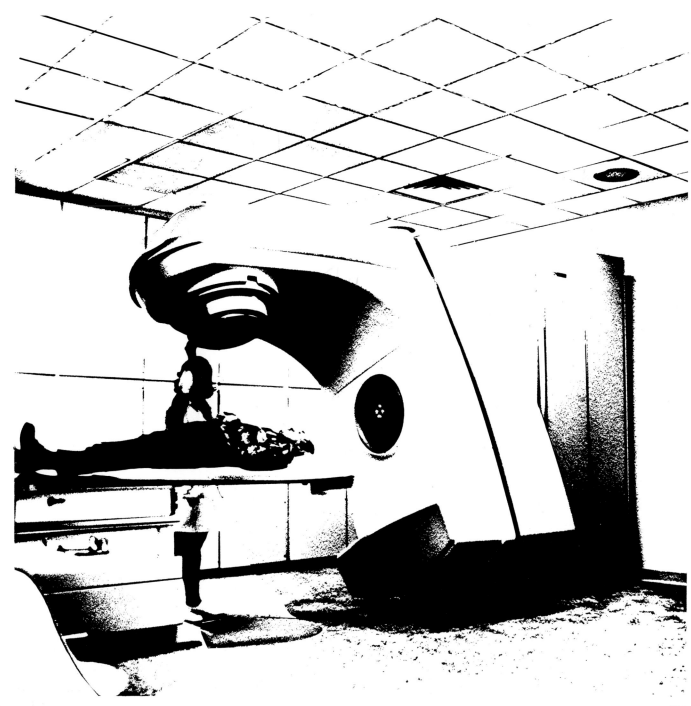

Trends in Health Care — Dallas Hospitals

James S. Wright, AIA

It is only within the last one hundred years that hospitals have been intended for other than the indigent sick and the war-wounded. Before that, any sick or injured person of reasonable means was treated and nursed back to health at home.

To counter this characteristic of hospitals, the Daughters of Charity of St. Vincent de Paul in 1896 converted a small cottage on Bryan and Hall Streets in Dallas into a hospital. Demand for care in their small haven was so intense (Dallas was approaching a population of 40,000) that only two years later they constructed Dallas's first real hospital. Built through donations on donated land near the cottage, the facility known as St. Paul Hospital began with 110 beds.

Sixty years later, having reached a capacity of 395 beds, the hospital on the old site was abandoned and a new 500-bed St. Paul Hospital was built on Harry Hines Boulevard.

Other important Dallas institutions began as church-related or charity hospitals, notably Baylor University Medical Center, Methodist Hospital, Presbyterian Medical Center, Gaston Episcopal Hospital, and Parkland Memorial Hospital. Today, those, along with a large new proprietary one known as Medical City Dallas, form the mainstay of that for which Dallas has become famous in the Southwest: highly specialized care for the acutely ill.

Physicians and hospitals in outlying towns send their more serious cases to these specialized institutions. The twenty-county North and East Texas area falls roughly into quadrants, each of which is served by one of the large city hospitals: the Northwest is served by St. Paul; the Northeast by Presbyterian and Medical City; the Southeast by Baylor; and the Southwest by Methodist Hospital.

Two unique, well known facilities have special service areas of their own. One is Parkland Hospital, the primary public-care institution, which is operated with countywide Hospital District taxes and thus absorbs most of the indigent and emergency cases from Dallas County. The other is the Texas Scottish Rite Hospital for Crippled Children. This hospital, which has evolved into a brand new thirty-million-dollar institution of considerable architectural merit, was the salvation of Texas children during the pre-1960s polio epidemics. Although it is a large project on a tight site, the architects have maintained human scale by breaking the mass into several well articulated elements that, through skillfully varied detailing, express clearly their inner functions.

Texas Scottish Rite Hospital for Crippled Children 1978
Harwood K. Smith & Partners

In size, Dallas facilities range from 1,125 beds in several buildings in the Baylor Medical Center Complex, to the 27-bed Medical Clinic at Southern Methodist University. Besides being large, Baylor has one of the greatest concentrations of medical skills and resources anywhere in the country and has an outstanding reputation for comprehensive care. (A note to football fans: Baylor is Cowboy headquarters for everything from the relief of pulled muscles to the surgical renovation of knees.) From the standpoint of patient load, however, Parkland is the undisputed leader; its volume of emergency and outpatient-clinic service is comparable with that of Cook County Hospital in Chicago. It was to this emergency facility that the Kennedy motorcade sped on November 22, 1963.

It has been said of hospitals that there can be no middle ground and that the hospital that does not move forward, changing to meet change, is moving backwards. In accord with the general prosperity of the area and the great Texas pride in progress, that pressing forward is perhaps more marked here than in other parts of the country.

Social influences have contributed to changes in hospitals. In seeking treatment for general or undiagnosed illnesses, people usually turn first to the hospital that is most convenient. The large central hospitals, left behind in deteriorating neighborhoods, have lost patients to new suburban hospitals. As a result, the quadrant hospitals have turned from dispensing "primary" care to giving highly specialized treatment requiring the greatest skill and the most advanced equipment. The large volume of cases referred from outlying, smaller hospitals is the life blood of the central hospitals.

In response to the need for primary care at the perimeter of the city, smaller hospitals have sprung up. Residents of most of the cities and towns surrounding Dallas have new community hospitals in which to enter the referral chain.

Some of the large central hospitals have built their own satellite hospitals. They provide convenience and avoid duplicating expensive services available at the parent hospital. Methodist Hospital pioneered this concept in Dallas County in 1973 with the satellite Charlton Methodist Hospital in far south Dallas County.

The unique character of certain inner-city neighborhoods has also influenced health care patterns. For example, the older but vigorously healthy and well defined community of near East Dallas is tightly knit, with long-standing loyalties to local retail establishments, physicians, and health services. Doctors Hospital, a progressive, hundred-bed, nonprofit institution outgrew their twenty-year-old building. Rather than desert the community for the suburbs, they built an impressive new 180-bed hospital and a multistory doctors' office building on a site they acquired right around the corner.

Baylor Medical Plaza Parking 1974
Harwood K. Smith & Partners
1975 AIA Dallas Award
Photo: Richard Payne

Left:
Baylor University Medical Center
Sammons Tumor Institute & Radiation
Center 1976
Harwood K. Smith & Partners

Methodist Hospitals of Dallas, Margaret Jonsson Charlton Branch 1975
Page Southerland Page

Doctors Hospital 1977
Page Southerland Page

Social changes have influenced not only the location and the intensity of service of Dallas hospitals, but the type of service as well. Ten years ago, ninety percent of diagnostic and treatment work was performed on patients who had been formally admitted to hospitals to stay for several days. Now, half the diagnostic radiology and clinical laboratory work in hospitals is performed on an outpatient basis. This has greatly affected the number of beds needed and the use of the beds that exist. Highly specialized quadrant hospitals are less affected by this because of the inherent seriousness and complexity of their cases.

Heart disease, bred by an increasingly well-fed, affluent, and labor-saved society, has generated highly specialized hospital services for both emergency and long-term treatment. Three central Dallas hospitals, Baylor, Parkland, and St. Paul, have open-heart surgery facilities, skills, and reputations second only to those in Houston and Palo Alto. As there is no other field in medicine in which proficiency is so closely associated with high volume, it is expected that these institutions will increasingly emphasize their heart skills, while other large hospitals will pursue different specialties, an example of unlegislated comprehensive health planning at its best.

The social change of working mothers and the unavailability of the after-hours physician has increased the demand for hospital services at odd hours. Emergency/outpatient departments are responding with seven-day twenty-four-availability. This, in turn, makes the health-care dollar go farther.

The influence of medical education on Dallas hospitals has significantly raised the quality of health care. Four quadrant hospitals, St. Paul, Methodist, Presbyterian, and Baylor, are affiliated with the University of Texas Southwestern Medical School, and each conducts residency programs under school supervision. Parkland, connected physically on all floors with the school, has as the chief of each department the corresponding faculty chief from the school. Teaching tends to pervade every aspect of hospital operation, and a positive attitude toward learning rubs off on both the resident physicians and the regular medical staff.

The University of Texas Health Science Center (formerly the Southwestern Medical School), a large complex of buildings, is an outstanding institution graduating two hundred new doctors each year. An indication of its national standing is the fact that of one hundred and five schools in the United States it has for the past five years been among the top three in terms of the National Board Examination scores posted by its graduates.

Architecturally, the recent buildings on campus are of unusually high quality, both in form and detail. Because of the University's penchant for passing around the work, each has been designed by a different architect, with the only apparent unifying design element being the color of the concrete.

Concern with consumer safety and the impact that increasingly stringent codes and standards have upon the design and cost of medical facilities is no greater in Dallas than elsewhere. One exception is that the Uniform Building Code used in Dallas requires all hospitals to have sprinkler systems throughout, except in certain electrically vulnerable patient areas. An increasing demand for energey efficiency has begun to modify some of the standards. For many years no recirculation of air was allowed in operating rooms, delivery rooms, and critical-care areas because of the possibility of concentrating explosive gases or infectious aerosols. Further research has shown that the standards could be relaxed at no loss of safety. Now highly efficient systems are used for filtering recirculated air and for evacuating anesthetic gases.

American Heart Association National Headquarters 1977 The Oglesby Group

Callier Center for Communication
Disorders 1965
Fisher & Spillman
1968 TSA Award
Aerial photo: Squire Haskins
Eye-level photo: John Rogers

In Dallas, as throughout the Sun Belt, the control of solar skin load is a major design factor that is resulting architecturally in more careful building orientation, less glass of higher performance, and exterior shading devices. There is a trend to a more widespread use of operable windows.

Advances in equipment technology are creating other pressures on hospitals. For example, radiology in Dallas began with a primitive diagnostic X-ray device installed at St. Paul Hospital in 1918. Machines have since become progressively larger and more complicated, providing a better image and requiring shorter patient exposure time. While X-ray movies for cardiac diagnosis have been used routinely for less than ten years, all principal hospitals in Dallas now have this sophisticated capability to examine what happens to blood as it flows through a beating heart.

Northlake Doctors Building 1966
Hallum & Wrightsman
Photo: John Rogers

143

Arlington Children's Clinic 1971
Pratt, Box, Henderson & Partners
1976 AIA Dallas Award
Photo: John Rogers

The most advanced piece of diagnostic equipment currently in vogue is the Computerized Axial Tomographic Scanner, developed in England by a research group spun off from The Beatles's original recording company. This machine is capable of visually "slicing" the body at any point, giving a minutely detailed image of a millimeter-thick cross-section. The scanner resembles a six-foot doughnut on edge. The patient is positioned in the "hole" on an attached table and the X-ray beam is rotated around him electronically. Exposure time is a matter of seconds, and because of its precision and speed, the technique is beginning to replace some of the more risky and painful diagnostic methods used for heart and brain work. Its advantages justify entirely the half-million-dollar price tag. The first machine in Dallas was acquired by Baylor University Medical Center, and in recent months CAT Scanners have been installed at six other Dallas hospitals.

Another trend affecting hospital design is that toward progressive patient care. It has always existed in Dallas hospitals in some form. The original 1898 St. Paul Hospital placed patients in its forty-bed Florence Nightingale wards according to the seriousness of their illness. Sicker patients were placed first nearest the Nurse Station and as they recovered were moved farther away.

Today, in Dallas as throughout the country, special care units have evolved. Coronary care is probably the best example. Typically, a patient is diagnosed initially with special equipment in the hospital emergency department and then transferred to a coronary care unit where he is monitored electronically and cared for by nurses who number better than one RN to every two patients. As his condition improves and the danger decreases, he is transferred to a post-acute coronary care unit. Here he has normal visitation privileges, but continues to be electronically monitored for danger signals, often by wireless telemetry. After he is judged recovered and is discharged, he can return for routine diagnosis and treatment to a minimal care unit. Here the cost is less and he can walk to the cafeteria and otherwise care for himself. Other special-care units such as the post-surgical

intensive care unit, the surgical recovery room, renal dialysis units, orthopedic extended-care units, stroke units, and day surgery units are all facets of progressive care in Dallas hospitals.

One facility, Presbyterian Medical Center, has carried progressive patient care even further, to a form that perhaps will set the pattern for future hospital care in the United States. Under the hospital's master plan now being implemented, the entire campus will be arranged for a true progression, from the diagnosis of illness through several levels of care, with the intensity of care fitted as nearly as possible to the gravity of the illness. Adjacent to the hospital is a professional office building. Here is the first link in the treatment chain, where the physician diagnoses the patient's illness with the help of either his own equipment or that of the hospital, depending upon the complexity of the procedure. From there the patient is either discharged or admitted to the acute-care hospital for short-term intensive and intermediate nursing care. At the proper time the patient is either discharged or admitted to a third element of the complex, which provides intermediate or sub-acute care. With this approach, costs to the patient are lower because less staff is required, yet the patient has access to all restorative services, and is cared for in a monitored environment.

Presbyterian now has broken ground for the final link in the chain of progressive patient care — the retirement center. Called Presbyterian Village North, this complex will contain retirement condominium units and a long-term nursing home, with backup support from the base hospital.

The Children's Development Center 1960
Pratt, Box, Henderson & Partners
1970 AIA Dallas Award
Photo: Balthazar Korab

The discipline of the dollar in medical facilities planning in Dallas has been consistently and uniquely strong. Both in cost per bed and in cost per square foot, Dallas hospitals are the lowest in the nation, being conceived first and foremost to fit a particular medical mission, with little investment in aesthetics. The principal institutions have generally been well planned, have functioned efficiently, and have accommodated reasonably well the requirements for change and growth; but, with few exceptions, they have been sited, shaped, and clad in the most economical fashion possible.

Strangely enough, funding of hospitals here still reflects the better times enjoyed formerly by other parts of the country. Public fund-raising is suffering nationwide, so that more and more there is a dependence upon hospital revenue and taxing bodies. However, in Dallas it still thrives and is the foremost means for hospitals to keep up with advancing technology and increasing demands for service. All the nonprofit institutions have phenomenal success with multimillion-dollar fund drives year after year, and they have continuing construction and development projects, either on campus or in the suburbs. This success in raising funds points up a sense of public responsibility for health care that appears to surpass that of Texas as a whole and indeed that of the United States.

Although there is a prevalence of charitably operated facilities in Dallas, there are also private for-profit hospitals playing a significant role in the health care delivery system. An example is Medical City Dallas, which with its modern facilities provides first-rate health care in a luxurious environment.

Dallas Lighthouse for the Blind 1975
Burson, Hendricks & Walls
Photo: David Williams

Mary Shiels Hospital
Phase One 1964: Dabney & Ramsey
Phase Two 1974: Aguirre & Dabney
Photo: James Lemkin

Washington-Worth Clinic 1965
Craycroft-Lacy & Partners
1965 TSA Award

Center right:
The Samuell Clinic 1965
Tie Davis-J. Murray Smith

Lower right:
Worth-Hill Clinic 1972
Craycroft-Lacy & Partners
1973 TSA Award
Photo: N. Bleeker Green

Richardson Professional Park 1966
The Pierce-Lacey Partnership

Changes in private medical practice have also influenced Dallas hospitals. Two-room offices above stores on Main Street have given way to chic, multiple-specialty office buildings adjacent to the physician's hospital-of-choice. The principal reason for the trend is economic: One additional hour of office time each day can raise a physician's income by 20 percent. The doctor has traded hours of driving back and forth from his office to various hospitals and nursing homes for a three-minute walk to the hospital elevator.

Typical of the medical office buildings are Wadley and Barnett Towers at Baylor, and buildings at Presbyterian, Medical City, St. Paul, and Doctors Hospital. All are multistory, with integral parking facilities, allowing convenient access from car to building. Doctors in those hospital-related offices generally concentrate on specialized care. To serve the primary-care needs of the population, there are active clusters of well designed physicians' offices in both the inner and the outlying areas. Typical are the Samuell Clinic off Harry Hines Boulevard near St. Paul Hospital, and the Mid-Cities Clinic in Grand Prairie, each accommodating progresive group practices of more than a dozen physicians. The Samuel Clinic is a nicely landscaped garden office building of residential scale, detailed softly in Mexican brick and natural wood; the Mid-Cities Clinic is a hard-edged, exposed concrete structure with a center court and a top-lighted waiting hall of near monumental scale.

Facilities that used to provide the downtown area with primary care have declined — choked by the cloud of dust from the stampede to the suburbs — and have started shutting down and relocating. The most recent move is that of the Medical Arts Hospital, which for 50 years occupied the top three floors of the Medical Arts Building at St. Paul and Pacific. It is now housed in new facilities on Harry Hines Boulevard, far from the city's center.

What does the future hold for health-care systems and facilities in Dallas? For one thing, the increasing life expectancy — the fact that persons over 65 years old soon will exceed 15 percent of the local population — will greatly increase the number of persons requiring skilled nursing care. For another, rising affluence will prompt more people to seek elective care when they need it, and this will increase caseloads.

The future may also see a moderation in the primary health care that is now being delivered mostly in the suburbs. Transportation problems and fuel costs will spur the redevelopment of older, close-in neighborhoods such as Oak Lawn. As more families move closer to downtown, the quadrant hospitals will again start delivering primary care.

Whatever the future holds, and whatever influences on health care prevail, it seems certain, if past performance is any indicator, that Dallas will remain at the forefront technologically, economically, and educationally.

Left:
The Meadowgreen 1972, a geriatrics center.
Olds-Udstuen-Thompson

Center left:
The Leaves Christian Science Sanatorium 1964
Woodward-Cape & Associates
1968 AIA Dallas Award

Lower far left:
Medical Arts Building 1922
C. E. Barglebaugh
Photo: Doug Tomlinson
This was reported to be the first office tower devoted specifically to the medical profession. It was razed in 1978.

Below:
Blanton Gardens 1964
Phase One: Fisher & Jarvis
Phases Two through Four: Jarvis Putty Jarvis
Aerial photo: Squire Haskins
Eye-level photo: John Rogers

147

Chapter 10
Cultural & Exhibition

Dallas — Showcase for the Nation

Ed E. Beran, AIA

Designing exhibition buildings will always be an exciting architectural challenge. Since the purpose of exhibit space is to display and sell, several requirements must be considered.

The space must be functional — large, open, and free of columns and adjunct facilities. It should be dramatic, but not overpowering. A building that overwhelms the displays is self-defeating.

The flow of traffic through the space is important — every tenant needs to be seen. The architect can satisfy this requirement by cleverly leading the viewer down well planned traffic lanes.

Lighting is important. Properly designed, it does not detract. A low level is desirable in passageways; this allows the eye to move to the display areas. Higher levels at strategic points can serve to direct traffic in predetermined directions.

Any well planned exhibit area will provide for human comfort. Looking at exhibits is tiring, so there must be conveniently accessible seating, lounges, food and beverages, first aid, and telephones. Graphics should be simple and attractive and directions clear.

The architect should take into account the excitement and bustle of the exhibit floor and plan for quiet havens where the visitor can rest, reflect, and experience a change of pace and surroundings. Atriums, plants, music, water — all help to create the necessary environment.

The first notable exhibition buildings in Dallas were perhaps those built in 1936 for the Texas Centennial Exposition at the State Fair. George Dahl was the Chief Architect, assisted by a team of ten Texas architectural firms; Paul P. Cret of Philadelphia was design consultant. Among the buildings were the Transportation Building, the Food and Fiber Building, the Agriculture Building, the Livestock and Poultry Building, the Federal Building, the Varied Industries Building, and the Hall of State. Some of the Exposition buildings, which are now considered to be the finest collection of Art-Deco structures remaining in the country, were built (at the unbelievably low cost of nine cents per cubic foot) to last only through the Exposition. Today, over forty years later, to the great credit of the architects and the builders, most of them are still being used as originally designed.

Right:
Fair Park
World Exhibits Building facing the Esplanade

Fair Park
World Exhibits Building 1936.
George Dahl, Chief Architect; Paul P. Cret, Philadelphia, Consulting Architect.
Photo: Dan Barsotti

Exhibition space in Dallas is sophisticated and efficient, and capable of serving groups large and small. Dallas is rapidly becoming known as an ideal convention city, and its Convention Center is one of the main reasons.

Everyone expects things in Texas to be big, and the Center is big, even by Texas standards. It contains 600,000 square feet of exhibit space and has the flexibility to accommodate 50 exhibitors or 1,500. The building has column-free rooms for aid in audio-visual presentations. Its 300-foot loading dock can handle forty trucks at a time. The seating capacity at the Exposition Hall (which is primarily an exhibit hall) is 28,000; banquet seating is 22,300. This attractive and efficient building is in a park-like setting near the center of downtown. The citizens of Dallas are justly proud of it and of the enormous amount of convention business it has attracted to the City. The architect for the original Memorial Auditorium was George Dahl. Recent additions were designed by Omniplan.

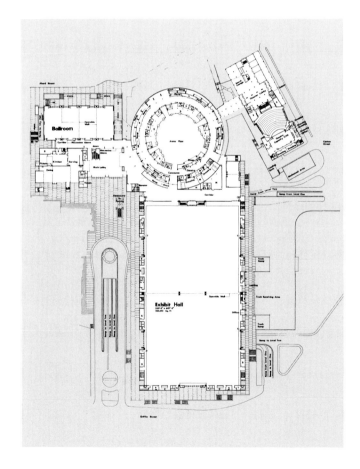

Above:
Dallas Convention Center 1973
Omniplan Architects Harrell + Hamilton
1974 AIA Dallas Award
1974 TSA Award
Photo: Geoff Winningham

Far left:
Dallas Convention Center & Memorial Auditorium Plan

Left:
Dallas Convention Center & Memorial Auditorium

Above:
Decorative Center 1955
Jacob E. Anderson
Later additions: Harold A. Berry

Lower right:
Trade Mart 1960
Harold A. Berry
The bridges are suspended from the roof structure.

Market Center
Photo: Squire Haskins

The innovative developer Trammell Crow and his associates have given Dallas something else to be proud of: the Dallas Market Center, considered to be the most beautiful and functional wholesale merchandise mart in the world. This is a 4.8-million-square-foot complex consisting of six buildings. Because of this remarkable center, Dallas now ranks as number one in the nation as a furniture market, floor-covering market, and gift market, and number two as an apparel market.

The Dallas Market Center is on 135 acres of landscaped grounds, and its buildings are enhanced by indoor gardens, courtyards, live birds, spiral stairways, skylights, and glass elevators.

The first buildings to be completed in the complex were the Decorative Center, begun in 1955 and now totaling 135,000 square feet. In this complex of buildings surrounding an open, tree-shaded square, the showrooms face latticed terraces, gardens, and malls. It is a functional place where buyers can select furniture, fabrics, and accessories for their clients.

The spacious Homefurnishings Mart, built in 1957, is one of the few buildings in the country built exclusively as a furniture mart. This 438,000-square-foot building was designed for the ultimate convenience and comfort of buyers, as well as for the most advantageous display of furniture.

The Trade Mart, built in 1959, contains approximately a million square feet. This building houses four floors of homefurnishings, gifts, floorcoverings, accessories, jewelry, toys, hardware, and housewares. The fifth floor is used solely as office space for the Market Center Company. The showrooms are built around a Grand Courtyard, which is four stories high and lighted by the sun.

Market Hall is one of the largest and finest privately owned exhibit halls in the country. Containing 214,000 square feet, it is an extremely functional building that may be used either in its entirety or divided into four separate halls, to serve exhibits of all kinds. It has efficiently accommodated national conventions, public and trade shows, carnivals, sports events, and automobile and boat shows, as well as major market and industry meetings. The seating capacity in the Exhibit Hall is 16,200 and banquet seating is 10,000.

The Apparel Mart, which opened in 1964, is the only building of its kind in the world. This unique, 1,334,592-square-foot building covers four city blocks and can efficiently house 1,650 fashion exhibitors under one roof. It provides showroom space that is convenient and beautiful as well as completely functional. The Great Hall, which was designed primarily for fashion shows, occupies the center portion of the building, with balconies overlooking it on each floor. It includes an acoustically perfect full working stage, with such features as natural plantings and a giant fountain whose water rises forty feet above the stage. The Great Hall easily accommodates 4,000 people for fashion events, and has a banquet seating capacity of 2,400. The building has a smaller Fashion Theater on the third floor for more specialized shows.

The architecture of the Apparel Mart is accented and enhanced by contemporary sculpture, fine tapestries of Bjorn Wiinblad, and a "Max Wall" — an entire wall of construction art created by Paul Maxwell.

Harold A. Berry was the chief architect for these first five buildings in the complex. Pratt, Box & Henderson designed the Great Hall at the Apparel Mart and the recently added West Atrium in that building.

The newest building in the Dallas Market Center is the exciting World Trade Center, which was dedicated on July 6, 1974, by then Vice President Gerald Ford. The addition of this building makes the center the largest wholesale merchandising complex in the world on one site. Presently the 1.4-million-square-foot building consists of seven floors; eight additional floors will be completed by 1980 on a foundation designed to carry twenty floors.

A 25,000-square-foot Hall of Nations forms the atrium of the World Trade Center. This tree-filled, seven-story courtyard is topped by a huge glass skylight. Colorful signal flags and flags from 67 nations exhibiting products at the Market Center accent the Hall of Nations, which is overlooked by balconies on the six floors above it. Only the first floor is open to the general public; buyers and manufacturers can reach the other floors by two glass capsule elevators.

This building connects with the Homefurnishings and Trade Marts, allowing buyers to shop all three buildings without going outside.

The World Trade Center was designed, as were all of the buildings in the Center, for maximum comfort and beauty, as well as efficiency. The architects for the World Trade Center are Beran & Shelmire.

The Dallas Market Center is indeed remarkable. Its buyers spend the incredible amount of over 4.5 billion dollars annually. Much of the credit for the success of this unique center is due to its far-sighted and imaginative developers, who put a great deal of thought and care into planning, with their architects, an environment that is not only efficient but aesthetically pleasing and thoroughly comfortable.

The Dallas/Fort Worth Airport, a major hub in the nation's transportation system, plays a key role in the development of Dallas as a national and an international market center. As more routes are added, trade increases. To meet the ever growing demand, exhibition space in Dallas will continually be expanded. The standards for exhibition buildings in Dallas have been high. There is reason to suppose that, with care on the part of architects and developers, they will continue in that tradition.

Above & near left:
World Trade Center 1974
Beran & Shelmire
1976 AIA Dallas Award
Photos: Jess Alford

Far left:
Apparel Mart Expansion 1973
Pratt, Box, Henderson & Partners
1974 AIA Dallas Award
Photo: James Lemkin

Below:
Great Hall of the Apparel Mart 1964
Pratt, Box, Henderson & Partners
1965 TSA Award
Photo: Balthazar Korab

THE KALITA HUMPHREYS THEATER
DALLAS THEATER CENTER

Dallas Theater Center 1959
Frank Lloyd Wright
1970 AIA Dallas Award
Photo: Linda Blase
Associated architects for the 1969
addition: William Wesley Peters, Taliesin
Associated Architects of the FLLW
Foundation; W. Kelly Oliver, Denver;
David George ·Reagan George; and
Newman ·Bradshaw. This was the only
public theater designed by Frank Lloyd
Wright.

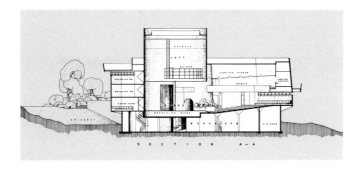

Far right:
Majestic Theater 1922
John Eberson, Chicago.
Photo: Doug Tomlinson
Restoration design studies are being made
by The Oglesby Group. Recently placed on
the National Register of Historic Places,
this theater originally was built for
vaudeville and was converted into a movie
theater during the 1930s. The City plans
to reconvert it to house live performances
of dance and drama.

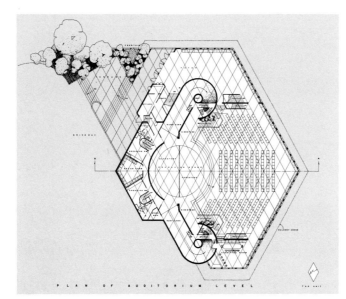

Fair Park

Terrell R. Harper, FAIA

The first and only public museum built in Dallas before 1936 was the Art Building at Fair Park; it was torn down in 1956. In 1936, Dallas hosted the Texas Centennial Exposition. On the 180-acre expanded site of the State Fair of Texas, six museums were constructed as the nucleus of the Exposition: the Hall of State, the Garden Center, the Health and Science Museum, the Aquarium, the Museum of Natural History, and the Museum of Fine Arts. All six are operating today, although the names of two of them have been changed. George L. Dahl of Dallas was the executive architect and Paul Philippe Cret of Philadelphia was design consultant.

Fair Park
View down the Esplanade, terminated by
the Hall of State.

Fair Park
World Exhibits Building
George Dahl, Chief Architect; Paul P.
Cret, Philadelphia, Consulting Architect.
Photo: Dan Barsotti

Far left:
Big Tex stands on the Fair Park grounds
during the annual State Fair of Texas.

Fair Park General
Development Plan
presented to the Dallas Parks Department
Board in 1971
Marvin Springer & Associates, Planners

The Hall of State is faced with Cordova cream limestone quarried in Central Texas. The main facade has a central dominating, concave entrace, flanked on each side by extensive wings. Statuary by Pompeo Coppini, and murals by Eugene Savage, enhance the Hall of Heroes and the Great Hall of Texas, respectively. The building, which cost $1.3 million, was at that time the most expensive structure per square foot ever built in Texas. Since 1938 the Dallas Historical Society has had its offices in the basement. The Society maintains the exhibits on the main floor, and serves as a research center for Texas historians. The collaborating architects for the Hall of State were Ralph Bryan, DeWitt & Washburn, Flint & Broad, Fooshee & Cheek, T. J. Galbraith, Anton Korn, Mark Lemmon, Walter Sharp, Arthur Thomas, and H. B. Thomson, all of Dallas, and Adams & Adams of San Antonio; Donald Barthelme was principal designer.

The Garden Center, originally called the Horticultural Museum, is of smooth, cream-colored brick with carved stone trim depicting the flora and fauna of Texas. It cost $220,000 to build. In 1971, Pratt, Box, Henderson & Partners were engaged to design an expansion in which specimen plants could be grown and displayed. This solarium is a steel-framed structure sheathed in clear glass set in a purposefully proportioned steel mullion system. Within the space are a number of vantage points to view the plants — overlooks, continuously sloping brick paths, and a mezzanine walkway. Lending the sight and sound of water are a waterfall and pool.

Far right:
Fair Park
Dallas Garden Center Solarium 1971
Pratt, Box, Henderson & Partners
1971 AIA Dallas Award
1971 TSA Award
Interior photo: Balthazar Korab
Exterior photo: David Connally

Right:
Fair Park
Hall of State 1936
Donald Barthelme, principal designer;
Ralph Bryan; DeWitt & Washburn; Flint
& Broad; Fooshee & Cheek; T. J.
Galbraith; Anton Korn; Mark Lemmon;
Walter Sharp; Arthur Thomas; H. B.
Thomson; and Adams & Adams of San
Antonio.
Photo: Doug Tomlinson

The Health and Science Museum, formerly called the Museum of Natural Resources and later the Museum of Domestic Arts, has an L-shaped plan and is faced with Cordova cream stone in ashlar pattern. Its severely simple lines are softened by Georgian and Colonial influences. The entrance, a semicircular portico with tall cut stone columns, suggests the Old South.

The Aquarium has a simple, rectangular plan 173 feet long and 88 feet deep. A rather ornate portico with high columns occupies the center of one long side. The otherwise plain walls on each side of the entrance are ornamented by carved stone sea horses. The cost of the building in 1936 was $155,000.

The Museum of Natural History is also of Cordova shell stone and is rectangular in plan. Three high openings at the main entrance admit the only natural light to the interior. The walls of the lobby are appropriately paneled in soft Cordova shell stone, a native Texas fossil stone. Its cost was $200,000.

The Museum of Fine Arts was originally a simple rectangle in plan, with one wing projecting on the south side. Faced with Cordova cream stone, and with a Harriet Frismuth fountain in the central court, the building was constructed at a cost of $500,000. It has since been expanded to almost double its original size. The addition, completed in 1963, was designed by Roscoe P. DeWitt. Edward Larabee Barnes of New York has been chosen as the architect to design a new Dallas Museum of Fine Arts, and he has designated the local architectural firm of Pratt, Box, Henderson & Partners to be associated with him on the project. However, the site for that museum has not yet been selected, nor its funding arranged.

Fair Park Music Hall
Lang & Witchell 1925
Renovation & addition 1972:
Jarvis Putty Jarvis
1974 AIA Dallas Award
Photos: John Rogers
Detailed as a Spanish Romanesque building, it served as the original Dallas Municipal Auditorium.

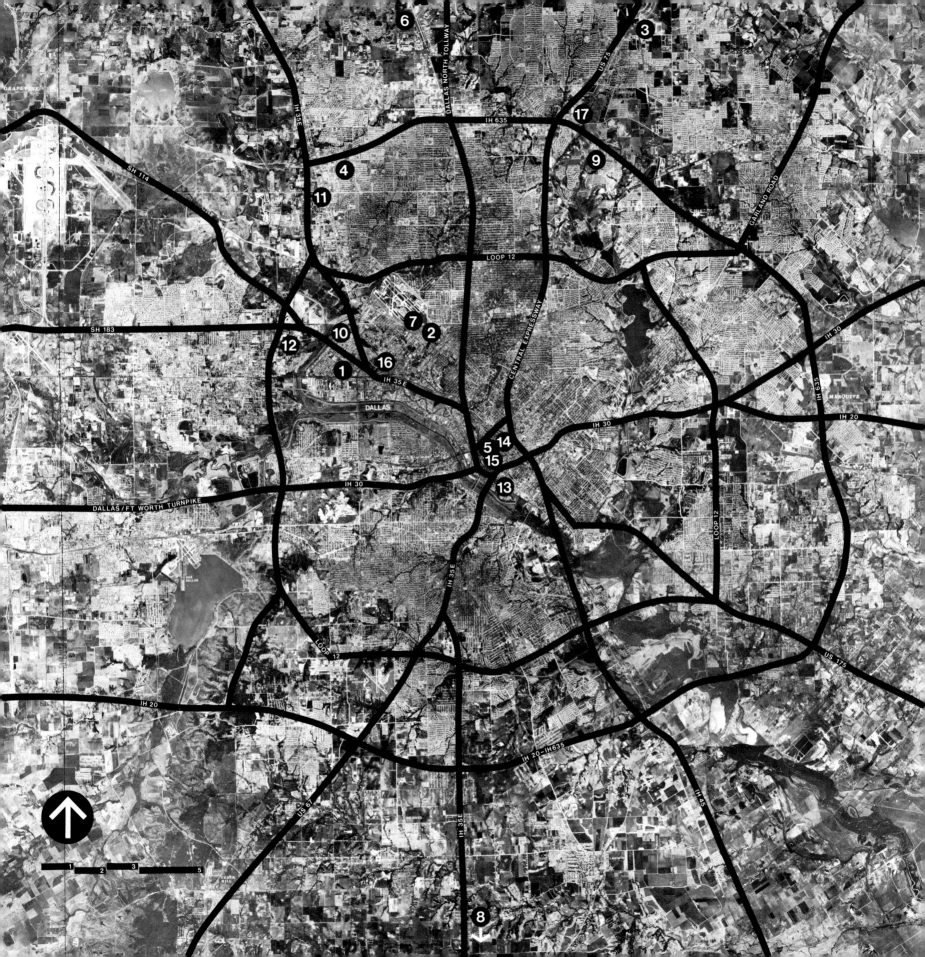

Chapter II
Industry

Edwards Manufacturing Co. c. 1901
Architect unknown
Restoration 1978:
Dahl, Braden, Chapman

Architecture For Industry: Dallas

David R. Braden, FAIA

Architecture for industry is unique in that its primary function is to conceive housing, and a suitable environment, for a machine or a manufacturing process. The emphasis on machine over man often produces "architecture" that is more often than not oriented toward engineering rather than architecture, and in the instance of heavy industry, the product can often be environmentally destructive to the community that sustains it.

Dallas has been blessed from an environmental standpoint in that its basic industrial forces have never been the kind that would seriously blight its landscape. In its beginning, Dallas emerged as a business center for cotton and oil, and later it blossomed into a regional and highly diversified commercial and industrial center. The city's inland location, the absence of a navigable river, and lack of mineral resources are the principal forces that have shaped Industrial Dallas and its architectural enclosures.

Dallas has never depended, nor had the opportunity to depend, on one or two dominant industries for growth and progress. We have neither Pittsburgh's steel nor Tulsa's oil, nor do we have New York's port. What we do have is diversity and a remarkable ability to adapt to the changing times and to the changing demands of the world's markets. Over the last thirty years, Dallas has developed as a recognized center for such "clean" industries as electronics, aerospace, and transportation.

There are a number of reasons for Dallas's industrial success: our attractive climate; a supportive banking and business community; an ample and well motivated labor market; excellent city government; a state right-to-work law; and a stable business, labor, and educational environment. These factors, plus the construction of the Dallas/Fort Worth Airport — the nation's "port of the future" — indicate that as an industrial leader Dallas will continue to maintain its position of prominence.

John Neely Bryan, whose log cabin rests on the Dallas County Courthouse Square, was undoubtedly Dallas's first manufacturer in that he made the first whiskey produced for sale. The architecture of the cabin indicates that it reflected more the construction practices of the time than it did Mr. Bryan's manufacturing operations.

By 1890, Dallas had attracted large businesses and industries that centered first in the area adjacent to the railroad terminal and the seat of Dallas County Government. This area, bounded by Elm and Lamar Streets and the MKT Railroad tracks, is still active in clothing manufacturing and warehousing. Many of Dallas's most historic buildings (circa 1900) are there, and it has recently been named a Historic District. Currently the area is undergoing intensive planning, and some buildings are already being remodeled. Eventually they will be adapted for commercial and residential purposes, as well as for manufacturing. The buildings are of both load-bearing-masonry and mill construction, and there are among them the first concrete-frame multistory structures in North Texas.

In 1973 a Historic Landmarks Preservation Committee was formed by the City to administer newly formed ordinances. The old warehouse district in downtown Dallas was designated a Historic District in 1976.

One of the more interesting buildings in the District is the three-story Edwards Manufacturing Company at 1800 North Market Street, an entirely functional concrete-frame building capped by a sheet metal Grecian cornice. The building has been adapted for use by the architectural firm of Dahl, Braden, Chapman; and a law firm occupies the top floor.

Out of the Historic District but still in the downtown area is another fairly early example of functional design for industrial purposes. The building at 710 North St. Paul, with its stepped-back floors, allowed north light to shine through glass roofs and walls for the purpose of sorting raw cotton. The light now finds its way to the drawing boards of its architect owners, The Oglesby Group. Four bold skylights on the roof light the offices of another architectural firm, The Pierce-Lacey Partnership.

In 1909, Dallas acquired its first Ford agency, and by 1913, local assembly of Ford automobiles had begun. By 1914, Ford had constructed an assembly plant at Canton and Henry Streets and was producing over 5,000 cars a year. Eleven years later, Ford completed a large assembly plant on East Grand Avenue, producing 350 automobiles and trucks per day. During World War II, the plant produced more than 100,000 trucks and Jeeps, and by 1968, the total production had exceeded three million vehicles.

The Ford assembly plant was, at best, nondescript, following the trend of the times in industrial architecture: Just put a roof over the machinery. It is interesting to note that it was its lack of flexibility — a common failing of industrial buildings of the period — that brought about the eventual closing of the plant; and no one has come up with an adaptive use for it. Although the plant had no architectural merit, it was in its day the largest industrial facility in the City. Later large industrial enterprises would devote far more attention to the architecture and planning both of plants and of their surroundings.

Dallas, which has no oil of its own, capitalized on supplying the supportive essentials of that industry. Thus we see in the City many buildings devoted to such oil-related enterprises as financing, legal services, geological and geophysical sciences, petroleum engineering, and oil-well equipment, but few that are for large-scale manufacturing or heavy industry.

710 N. St. Paul Building 1927
J. A. Japitzinger
Restoration 1970:
The Oglesby Group, Oglesby, Wiley, Halford
1971 AIA Dallas Award
1972 TSA Award

Southern Supply Co. 1911
J. Reilly Gordon & H. A. Overbeck
Photo: Doug Tomlinson
J. R. Gordon was known throughout Texas as the master of Romanesque. This building exemplifies the transition in Chicago School architecture from Richardsonian Romanesque to Sullivan's more attenuated skyscraper forms.

*Texts Instruments 1959-1968
O'Neil Ford, San Antonio, and Richard
Colley, Corpus Christi; A. B. Swank &
S. B. Zisman, Associated Architects.
Semi-Conductor Building 1961
1960 TSA Award
Photos: Rondal Partridge*

*On this five-hundred-acre site there is
more than three and a half million square
feet of building area. Interstitial space
(mechanical zones between floors) is
supported on V-tetrapods that were cast at
the site. That construction system is
unique to this project. TI is credited with
many electronic innovations such as the
integrated circuit and the "calculator on a
chip" which made electronic calculators
possible.*

Manufacturing in Dallas hit its stride with the coming of World War II, and by 1944 had achieved a peak of 75,600 manufacturing jobs. After the war, Dallas continued to add an average of seven thousand manufacturing jobs per year until 1970, and by 1973 had exceeded the combined growth rate of any three other cities in the Southwest.

Most of that phenomenal growth rate is attributable to the aircraft manufacturing industry and other businesses serving the military. Before the United States entered the war, North American Aviation of Inglewood, California, began constructing a large plant in the southwest part of Dallas County.

Although much can be said about the significance of this plant to America's war effort, it is important to note in any book concerned with architecture that the plant is equally significant in the industrial architecture of the nation. Here was a plant totally without historic cliches and pretensions, designed truly in the contemporary idiom to solve a contemporary problem.

The location was particularly favorable. It was placed inland to avoid surprise enemy attack and to spread the economic base of rearmament across the country. It was easily accessible to the highly productive and trainable labor markets of two fairly large cities, had plenty of space for expansion and change, and had, besides, the use of an adjacent military airfield.

To allow for manufacturing at night during war-time blackouts and to complement the completely controlled environment, the plant had no windows. Flexibility was created by the structural system, and the exterior materials were chosen for practicality and speed of erection rather than for aesthetic purposes. Fluorescent lighting was used to achieve the most efficient lighting levels and to complement energy factors. In short, by previous standards, the contemporary architect and his functional approach to design had made a significant contribution to industrial architecture in Dallas.

Texas Instruments Semi-Conductor Building during construction. Photo: N. Bleeker Green

The building stands as a monument to the importance of flexibility as a design criterion in architecture for industry. After the departure of North American Aviation, it became the base of operations for Texas Engineering & Manufacturing Co. (TEMCO) and Chance Vought Aircraft, whose subsequent merger produced the giant multiple-industry conglomerate, LTV Corporation.

These companies not only stimulated real-estate and commercial fields, but also spawned an array of light manufacturing industries that included machine shops, processing and plating shops, tool and die makers, and sheet-metal fabricators.

The designs for these major industrial plants came from the drawing boards of architects outside the local architectural community. However, as the community grew, so did the architectural resources of the area, so that soon local architects began to serve the burgeoning industries of the region.

Two of the most important plants in the area were designed by local firms. Texas Instruments, on North Central Expressway, was designed by O'Neil Ford and Richard Colley, with A. B. Swank as Associated Architect, and the LTV Aerospace Center, on West Jefferson, was designed by George L. Dahl, Architects and Engineers.

Texas Instruments, a pioneer in the electronic transistor field, had only a basic design for those tiny components when it discovered the technique of producing them in the quantities needed to make solid state electronic equipment economically competitive with the vacuum tube. In spite of intense competition from Japan, TI continues to be a leader in the complex electronics industry. The plant is a one-of-a-kind exercise in award-winning contemporary architecture, employing the structural innovation of concrete hyperbolic forms to achieve the utmost in industrial efficiency with a high level of visual and environmental qualities for its employees and visitors.

The LTV Aerospace Center was produced by fast-track design and construction techniques before the term was even invented. This highly flexible and pleasant place to work has played a large role in America's space program. The building groups both corporate offices and industrial employee dining and recreational space around a courtyard of fountains and greenery.

Since World War II, Dallas has developed sizable districts for light manufacturing and warehousing, served to varying degrees by rail, truck, and air transportation. From them have poured forth electronic calculators, optical scanners, microwave products, and radio, television, and stereo components.

Dallas's earliest Post World War II industrial district, along the banks of the Trinity River, was a travesty. It was so poorly planned that it served as a significant contribution to the art: It was so bad that it inspired others to do better! The planned industrial districts that followed it, and the plants they contain, should be seen by anyone interested in functional industrial architecture of high quality. They include the Brook Hollow District, Great Southwest District, Redbird Industrial Park, and the latest one, Las Colinas Corporation (planned by Ernest J. Kump Associates of California).

Significant manufacturing plants in the area include Varo, Inc., on Kingsley Road in Garland, producers of high-voltage rectifiers used by many of America's principal makers of television receivers; the Frito-Lay complex at 900 North Loop 12; Recognition Equipment, on Grauwyler Road in Irving; and Taylor Publishing Co. on West Mockingbird Lane, one of the world's leading printers of school yearbooks.

The Mary Kay Cosmetics plant on Carpenter Freeway represents Dallas's entry into the production and distribution of health and beauty aids on an international level. Mary Kay, Inc., is a home-grown company that has rapidly achieved leadership in its field. The plant employs a unique controlled environment for the manufacture of its products.

Top left:
Sculpture by Roger Bolomey at the entrance of Northgate Industrial Park.

Top right:
Sears Roebuck & Co.
Catalog Order Warehouse 1972
Harper & Kemp
Photo: W. D. Smith

Above:
Brookhollow Industrial District 1954
Initially developed with 1200 acres. The Urban Land Institute refers to this park as a textbook example of industrial land planning.

Far right:
Recognition Equipment 1970
Pratt, Box, Henderson & Partners
1971 TSA Award
Photo: Doug Handel

Jetrail Parking Terminal
Braniff International 1970
The Pierce-Lacey Partnership
1971 AIA Dallas Award
1971 TSA Award

Upper left & above:
Mary Kay Cosmetics, Inc., 1977
Dahl/Braden/Jones/Chapman

Left:
Taylor Publishing Company 1966
Harwood K. Smith & Partners
1968 AIA Dallas Award
Photo: John Rogers

167

Eastman Kodak Regional
Distribution Center 1970
Harwood K. Smith & Partners
1971 TSA Award
Photos: John Rogers

Above:
Liquid Paper Company 1975
Neuhaus + Taylor

Coca-Cola Bottling Co. 1963
Pitts, Phelps & White, Beaumont

Kerr Container Plant 1967
Beran & Shelmire
1968 AIA Dallas Award
1970 AIA Dallas Award
1968 TSA Award
Photo: John Rogers
The sidewalls of the furnace building
overhang the grade beam to accommodate
hinged fresh-air vents. The original client
was the Armstrong Cork Company.

There are now in Dallas a number of architectural and engineering concerns that deal on a national level with architecture for industry. They are innovators, and as such have greatly raised the level of planning — promoting functionalism and flexibility, which are indispensable to any industrial-use facility. A major contribution of these firms has been to give to places of production that which they have almost always lacked before: well-thought-out aesthetic and environmental qualities.

Dallas faces many challenges. It has become the eighth largest city in the nation and with Fort Worth combines to be the tenth largest marketing area. Light manufacturing is on the increase. Among persons employed in those routine and mundane jobs there is a rising assertion that they deserve better surroundings. This calls for a sensitive response from both architects and employers. Good design is good business: It promotes higher productivity and makes for employee stability, both of which are criteria for good management. The importance of building and strengthening a community of architects skilled in industrial-facility design cannot be overestimated.

Upper far left & above:
Forney Engineering Company 1972
Beran & Shelmire
1975 AIA Dallas Award
1974 TSA Award
Photos: Jess Alford
The plant contains a child care center for the employees' children. The principal exterior material is insulated steel panels that are removable for future expansion.

Center left:
Collins Radio Company
Headquarters Office Building 1966
Harper & Kemp
Photo: John M. Couch

Lower left:
Opticks, Inc., 1969
Harwood K. Smith & Partners
Photo: John Rogers

Chapter 12
The Region

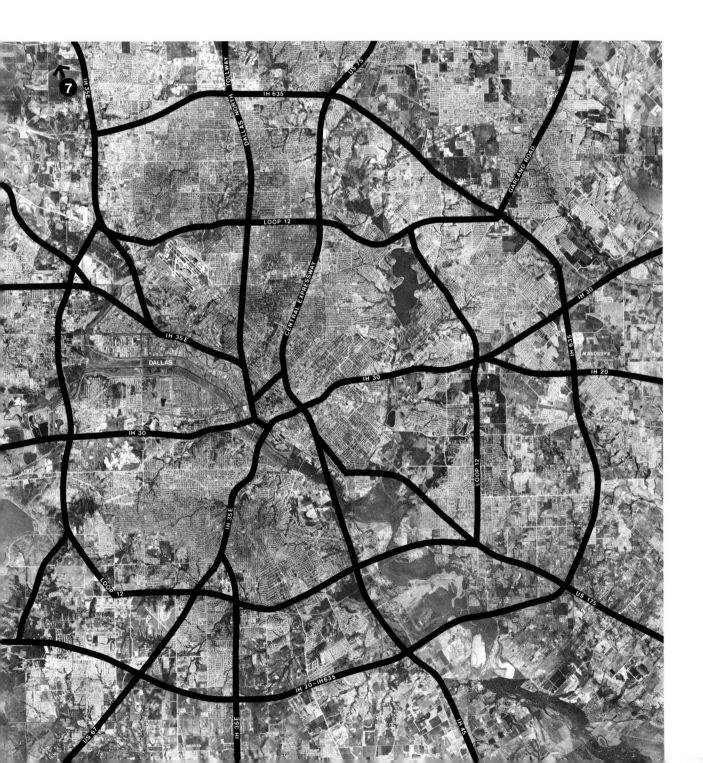

1. Amon Carter Museum of Western Art
   3501 Camp Bowie Boulevard
2. Dallas/Fort Worth Airport
   Highway 183 & International
   Parkway
3. Downtown Fort Worth
   a. First National Bank of Fort Worth
      500 W. 7th & Lamar
   b. Flatiron Building
      Houston Street & Ninth
   c. Fort Worth Municipal Building
      1000 Throckmorton & Tenth
   d. Fort Worth National Bank
      500 Throckmorton & Fifth
   e. Tandy Center
      Throckmorton at First & Third
   f. Tarrant County Courthouse
      Main & Houston
   g. Water Gardens
      Houston Street & 17th
4. Fort Worth Art Museum
   1309 Montgomery & Camp Bowie
5. Fort Worth Botanical Gardens
   University Avenue & IH-20
6. Kimbell Art Museum
   Will Rogers Road West & Camp
   Bowie Blvd.
7. North Texas State University, Denton
   a. Art Building
   b. Coliseum
   c. Student Union Building
8. Penn Street Residences
9. Residence, Westover Hills
10. Residence, Westover Hills
11. Saint Andrews Catholic Church
    3717 Stadium Drive
12. Sid Richardson Science Building
    Texas Christian University
13. Stockyards Historic District
    N. Main Street & Exchange
14. Tarrant County Junior College
    Northwest Campus
    4801 Marine Creek Parkway
15. Thistle Hill
    1509 Pennsylvania at Summit
16. University of Texas at Arlington
    a. Business Administration Building
    b. Fine Arts Building

Fort Worth — The Companion City

Alan R. Sumner, AIA

From the very founding of Camp Worth in 1848, the thirty miles that separates Dallas and Fort Worth has gradually succumbed to urban sprawl. Although the distance between the two cities has, of course, remained constant, the physical appearance has slowly changed to reflect the population growth. Both cities have themselves expanded dramatically, and the space between them is punctuated by the edges of the Mid-Cities — Arlington and Grand Prairie. Irving, another large suburb, is just north of Grand Prairie and west of Dallas. In driving the Dallas/Fort Worth Turnpike, one senses the presence of those suburbs. But one never actually sees them as cities; to do so requires leaving the Turnpike. Hurst, Bedford, and Euless, other growing suburbs, can be seen from Highway 183, the northern east-west corridor. Most of the residents of those cities commute to work — eastward to Dallas or westward to Fort Worth. Many of the suburbs have populations easily exceeding 200,000, and they are steadily coming together into one great urban blanket.

Fort Worth deserves attention both as a city and as the site of some notable architecture. Its early history, too, is exciting and worth going into, however briefly.

Fort Worth was established as an army outpost in 1849, a few years after Dallas was founded. Major Ripley Arnold named the camp after his recently deceased commander, General William J. Worth, a man who had distinguished himself in the War of 1812 and as a commandant of West Point. General Worth had sent Major Arnold north from San Antonio to command the two northernmost forts in a line of new forts that had been built to protect San Antonio, Austin, Waco Village, and Dallas, at the western edge of the frontier. Four years later, as the frontier moved west a hundred miles with a new line of forts, Fort Worth was abandoned as a military post.

But it formed the nucleus of a town. Although it suffered from Indian raids, and the population dwindled during the Civil War, it managed to survive and finally to revive.

Economic stimulus came in the form of cattle. Hundreds of thousands of head had been driven from Fort Worth northward up the Chisholm Trail and from Dallas northward up the Shawnee Trail into Missouri long before the Civil War. Most were trailed to St. Louis and Chicago, some as far as New York City. In 1858, a widespread outbreak of Texas Fever brought quarantines that effectively closed the Shawnee Trail to Texas cattle. Dallas, located on the Shawnee Trail, lost its opportunity to become "Cowtown." But the Plains provided another source of income: the American buffalo. Hides fetched a dollar apiece. During the height of the great buffalo slaughter, more than 200,000 hides were transported through Fort Worth alone.

From 1865 to 1868, the population of Fort Worth doubled. It doubled again in 1872 in anticipation of the coming railroad. In 1873, the Texas Legislature enacted the bill that incorporated the City of Fort Worth.

Sculpture by Sir Henry Moore and a specimen mesquite tree form an unexpected foreground composition in Will Rogers Memorial Center. This view, from the Amon Carter Museum, stretches across the valley of the West Fork of the Trinity River toward the skyline of downtown Fort Worth.

The effect of the Panic of 1873 on Fort Worth was disastrous: The New York Stock Exchange closed for ten days and the market for cattle dried up. Then a killing blizzard swept through the cattle country. To make matters worse, the Texas and Pacific Railroad stopped laying track thirty miles short of Fort Worth. Dallasites, who already had their railroad, found humor in Fort Worth's plight, expressing as much in a number of newspaper articles. To reverse the situation, a group of Fort Worth citizens formed a construction company to complete the railroad beds so the railroad could continue into town. Tenacity and hard work got the job done, but the neighboring towns of Sherman and Dallas viewed with amusement these efforts they considered piecemeal.

In 1878, Fort Worth became the easternmost point of the world's longest stagecoach line, a 1,560-mile route ending in Yuma, Arizona. Fort Worth was now the railhead and the passenger center for West Texas. In 1880 and 1881 two more railroads arrived, and once again the economy was bolstered.

During the 1870s, Fort Worth struggled with the typical western-town dilemma: what to do with the cowboys, freighters, buffalo hunters, and railroad men. There developed a section of town known as Hell's Half Acre, boasting bars, sporting houses, dance halls, and shooting galleries. It operated wide open twenty-four hours a day. The merchants needed the cowboys to survive economically, so rather than close down the area, they chose to tolerate Hell's Half Acre, with limitations. To administer the law with a light touch, the town elected "Long Hair Jim" Courtright marshal. Before coming to Fort Worth, Courtright had been a scout in the Civil War, companion scout with Wild Bill Hickock in the Indian Wars, and a performer with Buffalo Bill Cody and Annie Oakley. He served as marshal from 1876 until 1879, and ended his life in a classic shootout with the gambler Luke Short in 1887.

During the next few years, George Leroy Parker and Harry Longbaugh, better known as Butch Cassidy and The Sundance Kid, lived in Fort Worth. With their "Wild Bunch" they robbed trains and banks all over the southwest and northwest. Eventually the Union Pacific Railroad had their fill of Butch and Sundance and hired The Pinkerton Agency to track them down. Desperadoes like those, and an increasing number of murders, finally became intolerable and Hell's Half Acre was shut down.

The 1880s were good years for Fort Worth. The town got its first water system, its first public schools, and a full-time district court. An opera house opened; and an electric streetcar line was begun, the second in the nation. When the railroads became well established and cattle could be shipped to market, the great trail drives came to an end. Cattlemen moved their headquarters to the City. The famous Stockyards were established, and later also the meatpacking plants. Through the efforts of thirty citizens who contributed $10,000 each, the Fort Worth Dressed Meat and Packing Company was founded. Swift & Company and Armour soon followed.

Right:
Flatiron Building 1908
Sanguinet & Staats, Fort Worth
This is a reasonable imitation of
Burnham's New York skyscraper of the
same name.

Tarrant County Courthouse 1894
One of a number of fine North Texas
county courthouses in the neo-Romanesque
style.

Fort Worthians, feeling their oats, wanted to focus attention — both national and international — on their city. They would stage a national exposition. Captain Buckley B. Paddock, editor of the *Fort Worth Democrat,* was instrumental in raising the money to build the Fort Worth Spring Palace. This fairy-castle exhibition hall, measuring 225 feet by 375 feet, was in the shape of a Saint Andrew's cross and had a dome 150 feet in diameter, surpassed in size only by that of the nation's capitol. The Palace opened May 10, 1889. A little more than a year later a fire of unknown origin destroyed the entire building in eleven minutes.

Misfortunes notwithstanding, Fort Worth became more and more a city. Texas Wesleyan University was founded in 1881. A new courthouse was built in 1894. In 1910, Texas Christian University settled there permanently. Fort Worth became the merchandising center for West Texas. Hospital facilities expanded. The city's first large hotel, The Worth, was built in 1894 — and stood until it was demolished in January 1978. The Fort Worth Opera House boasted such performers as Lilly Langtry, Edwin Booth, Lillian Russell, Sarah Bernhardt, Douglas Fairbanks, and the Barrymores, Ethel, Lionel, and John.

By 1900 the population of Fort worth exceeded 70,000. The city was ready for the twentieth century. In *How Fort Worth Became the Texasmost City* (published in 1973), Leonard Sanders refers to that period in Fort Worth's history as the awakening. Aviation, oil, and the military establishment were the governing factors.

Fort Worth contrasts

Where the West is.
The Stockyards District developed in the twenty years following 1902, as a number of large packing houses located in the town of Niles City. Today, the covered boardwalks of North Main and Exchange look like a movie set, yet all is authentic. Fort Worth grew upwind of this area and left the north side to reminisce on another day.

Fort Worth today is a fascinating blend of local Old West and sophisticated urbanity — Cowtown gone Uptown. The western heritage is highly visible and prevalent. Cowboy boots and Stetson hats are as much at home in downtown banks and stores as they are in the historic Stockyards. Money amassed from a local newspaper funded an unexcelled collection of Western art and housed it in a building designed by an internationally renowned architect. The Casa Mañana Theater, with its shining geodesic dome by R. Buckminster Fuller was the first permanent arena in America built expressly for the presentation of musical shows.

Fort Worth has an impressive number of well planned open spaces and exceptional buildings. In the southwest corner of Trinity Park are fifty acres of rolling lawns, natural forest, spring-fed lagoons, and formal and informal plantings that constitute the Fort Worth Botanic Garden. Six acres of this have been developed into a charming Japanese Garden. In one large "park," part of the 32-acre Centennial Exposition Grounds, are three art museums: the Fort Worth Art Museum, earliest of the group; the Amon Carter Museum of Western Art; and the Kimbell Art Museum. The Fort Worth Art Museum houses a collection of contemporary art.

The Amon Carter Museum of Western Art, currently being enlarged to accommodate a growing collection of pre-1950 American art, was originally built for Amon Carter's large collection of Russell and Remington paintings and sculptures. The architect was Philip Johnson. The original building appears as simple as a Greek temple. The smoothly shaped columns taper into arches that support a flat roof. The exterior material is quarried shellstone. On the interior a combination of bronze, teakwood, and shellstone provides an appropriate setting for Western art. This finely detailed museum faces east toward its neighbor across the park, the Kimbell Art Museum.

Kimbell Art Museum 1972
Louis I. Kahn, Philadelphia;
Preston M. Geren & Associates,
Fort Worth, Associated Architects.

Lower left:
"You know what's so wonderful about the porches? They're so unnecessary."
Louis Kahn
Photo: Bob Wharton

Below:
"The museum has as many moods as there are moments in time."
Louis Kahn

The Kimbell Art Museum, one of the last buildings designed by Louis Kahn, defines the eastern edge of the park. This dynamic structure encloses 120,000 square feet of column-free space. A series of cycloid vaults, each with slits in the center, sides, and exterior ends, defines the roof. The play of natural light through these openings makes the vaults appear weightless. Kahn's structural message is clear: the supportive structure is of exposed concrete and the nonsupportive is sheathed in marble.

Westover Hills, much like the Park Cities in Dallas, was an island city created to protect property values and preserve a high quality of living. These houses are on one of that town's wooded hillsides.

Residence 1973
I.M. Pei & Partners, New York

Residence 1975
Paul Rudolph, New York

Other notable architects of national reputation have been sought by Fort Worth citizens. Edward Durell Stone designed the City Hall in downtown Fort Worth. In this building, of a strongly horizontal shape, the offices are oriented around a central open space with a fountain. The First National Bank of Fort Worth is indicative of the early 1960s style of Skidmore, Owings & Merrill. The vertical and horizontal structure is clearly defined, with the glass tucked away from the bright Texas sun. A granite sculpture by Isamu Noguchi stands near the main entrance. I. M. Pei was commissioned to design a Fort Worth residence. Around the corner from the Pei house is one designed by Paul Rudolph.

Paul Rudolph also designed the Sid W. Richardson Physical Sciences Building on the campus of Texas Christian University. In this building, designed in 1969 in association with Preston M. Geren of Fort Worth, the buff-tan brick of the existing, traditionally styled campus buildings is deftly used to express the excitement of twentieth century architecture. A series of dynamic spaces is defined by oval columns, horizontal lines, and projecting planes.

*Tarrant County Junior College
Northwest Campus 1976
Preston M. Geren & Associates,
Fort Worth
TCJC, like its Dallas counterpart, has
developed a reputation for outstanding
architecture. This campus is one enormous,
rambling structure on the shores of Marine
Creek Lake.*

*Coliseum 1974
North Texas State University
Clutts & Parker*

*Right:
Student Union Building 1976
North Texas State University
Jarvis Putty Jarvis*

*Upper far right:
Art Building 1972
North Texas State University
Clutts & Parker*

*Fine Arts Building 1974
University of Texas at Arlington
Parker-Croston Associates, Fort Worth*

*Right:
Business Administration Building 1977
University of Texas at Arlington
Albert S. Komatsu & Associates,
Fort Worth
Photo: T. E. Stewart*

*Lower far right:
St. Andrews Catholic Church 1970
Albert S. Komatsu & Associates
Photo: Phillip Poole*

John Portman of Atlanta designed the Fort Worth National Bank, which opened in 1973. This thirty-nine-story building has a square plan with flattened or beveled corners that flare into a pyramidal base at the street. A bright red-orange forty-foot-tall steel stabile "Eagle" by Alexander Calder stands guard at the foot of the building. Upon entering, one finds oneself on a bridge spanning the banking floor, which lies below street level. Above is the circular employee cafeteria. The space is larger, airier, sunnier, and deeper than expected.

An outstanding addition to Fort Worth is the Fort Worth Water Garden by Philip Johnson and John Burgee of

New York City. In 1974 the Amon G. Carter Foundation commissioned them to design this gift to the City. Near the highly active Convention Center, this Water Garden serves as an oasis in the city and a new focal point. The park encompasses four and a half city blocks of extravagant water works. Diversity of water flow defines the individual areas. A Central Plaza separates the Aerating Pool with its forty nozzles from the Quiet Pool. The latter, far below street level, is reached by stairs projecting from battered exposed-aggregate walls. Smooth sheets of water feed the tree-rimmed Quiet Pool. Across the Plaza is the spectacular Active Pool. Rimming this pool is a trough seven hundred

Far left:
Fort Worth National Bank 1974
John Portman & Associates, Atlanta;
Preston M. Geren & Associates,
Fort Worth.

Interior:
With his usual verve for spatial excitement,
Portman created a lobby to make visitors
stop and look around.

Fort Worth Water Gardens 1976
Johnson/Burgee, New York
Below & left:
The Active Pool
Bottom:
Foreground, The Quiet Pool

and twenty feet long, from which a continuous sheet of water cascades down tiers thirty-eight feet below grade. Oversized steps permit the visitor to descend along the cataracts to the bottom. The south side of the park is defined by the highest point, the Concrete Mound. A series of irregularly angled tiers of concrete and planting provides an overlook of the entire intriguing water display.

The confines of this essay do not allow for a full treatment of all the City's worthy buildings and planned spaces. Fort Worth — its history, its character, and its architecture — deserves a book of its own.

181

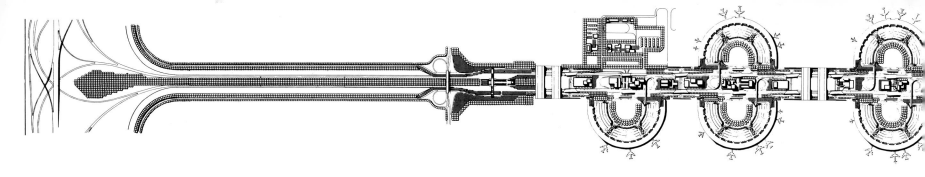

Precast concrete is used consistently throughout the airport buildings and roadway elements. Rails and poles are oxidizing steel. Graphics are in a sedate brown.
Photo: Kiku Obata

Above far right:
Airplane photo: Courtesy Dallas Chamber of Commerce

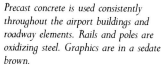

Terminal interior
Photo: Stephen Dunham
       Kiku Obata
Photo, right: Barbara Martin

Dallas/Fort Worth Airport 1973
Hellmuth, Obata & Kassabaum, St. Louis;
Brodsky, Hopf & Adler, New York;
Associated Architects
Omniplan Architects Harrell+Hamilton;
Preston M. Geren & Associates,
Fort Worth
1977 AIA Dallas Award

Fort Worth and Dallas are interrelated. The two cities form a significant metropolitan region with an ever-growing population that currently exceeds 2.8 million. The eleven-county Standard Metropolitan Statistical Area of which they are a part is now the largest inland SMSA in the United States.

Dallas and Fort Worth have always competed with each other. First cattle, then railroads, then oil, aviation, and electronics. Each city retains its distinct identity, but a new maturity has emerged. An intercity cooperation has been fostered to achieve goals that otherwise would be unattainable. A symbol of that cooperation is the Dallas/Fort Worth Regional Airport, on a 17,500-acre site straddling Dallas and Tarrant Counties. In moving this region into the forefront of air travel, the two cities eventually will have spent over a billion dollars. More than forty thousand people will have been employed. It will be an airport larger than Manhattan Island — over nine miles long, and at its widest point, eight miles across. In a truly Texas tradition, Dallas and Fort Worth have combined forces to produce the largest airport in the United States and the second largest in the world.

Both cities are willing to participate in joint ventures that greatly benefit the entire region, and the Mid-Cities enjoy the ripple effect.

Fort Worth is a unique city. Dallas is a unique city. Together they should form the nucleus of the finest urban region in America. The determination that has brought them this far from their Early West beginnings will carry them as leaders into the twenty-first century.

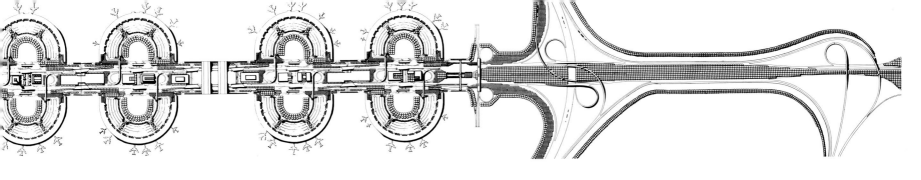

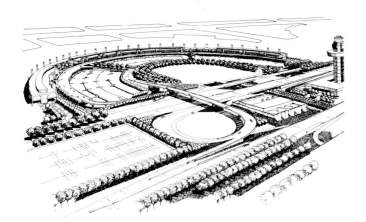

Decentralized terminal facilities minimize the distance a traveler walks between automobile and airplane. The semicircular terminal units are linked by a spine road and a computerized people mover. Aircraft park on the outside, automobiles on the inside of each loop.
Photo: Barbara Martin
Drawings: Myrick-Newman-Dahlberg

Project Index

Sculpture Index